AND
SO
IT IS

DAILY
AFFIRMATIONS
GUIDE
USING THE 369
METHOD
FOR HIM

Sweet Inspirations for the Soul
- Affirming, Attracting, and
Embracing your Limitless Self.

JOYCE LICORISH

AND SO IT IS

DAILY AFFIRMATIONS GUIDE USING THE 369 METHOD FOR HIM

Sweet Inspirations for the Soul - Affirming, Attracting, and Embracing your Limitless Self.

JOYCE LICORISH

TABLE OF CONTENTS

TABLE OF CONTENTS

This book is Book 1 in the And So It Is Book Series by Author Joyce Licorish

AND SO IT IS:
DAILY AFFIRMATIONS GUIDE
USING THE 369 METHOD FOR HIM
DREAMEMPIRE
PAPERBACK ISBN:979-8-9876367-6-3

For Author Appearances or Bookings visit
www.RenitaJHills.com

DreamEmpire Publishing
3775 Venture Drive
Bldg A Suite 202 Duluth, GA 30096
www.dreamempirepublishing.com

INTRODUCTION

Welcome to "And So It Is - Daily Affirmations Guide Using the 369 Method for Him" a book focused on honing in on Strength, Clarity, and Purpose for the Modern Man. This book is more than just a journal—it's a voyage into the core of your being, a transformative path that empowers you to seize the power of positive affirmations and unleash the vast, untapped potential that defines you.

Life presents its fair share of obstacles and uncertainties. At times, these challenges might make us question our path or feel detached from our authentic selves. Yet, beneath these fleeting doubts, there's an unyielding wellspring of resilience, purpose, and wisdom within every man. This guide is your key to unlocking that reservoir and truly understanding the formidable force that you are.

Within these pages lies a set of affirmations meticulously tailored for the modern man. They push beyond the conventional "I am" statements, aiming to bolster your confidence, ignite your drive, and shift your perspective. It's our firm belief that the right affirmations can not only reshape your self-view but can also redefine how you interact with the world.

Engage with these powerful affirmations, and you'll find yourself on a self-realization quest. You'll reaffirm the strength, ambition, and determination inherently present within you, recognizing that you're the master of your destiny with the capability to manifest your aspirations.

Consider this book a reliable ally on your daily journey toward self-betterment. Dedicate a few moments each day to reflect on these affirmations, internalizing their truths. Embrace their transformative nature, and observe the myriad of positive changes that transpire in your life.

Navigating through "Strength, Clarity, and Purpose for the Modern Man", remember you're backed by a brotherhood, a global community of men striving for betterment. Together, our collective energy can spark a movement of growth and positive transformation.

So, fellow traveler, take a moment, focus your mind, and let these affirmations steer you toward the boundless version of yourself. Here's to the journey ahead!

With love and light,

Joyce Licorish

Author of the 'And So It Is' Book Series

ACCOUNTABILITY CHECK

CONSISTENCY MATTERS

"Small disciplines
repeated with
consistency every day
lead to great
achievements gained
slowly over time."

JOHN C. MAXWELL

ACCOUNTABILITY CHECK

Consistency in journaling can be a transformative habit. When we commit to chronicling our thoughts, emotions, and experiences each day, we create a powerful tool for reflection and growth. Being accountable for this daily practice ensures that we capture the nuances of our journey, helping us recognize patterns, celebrate achievements, and understand setbacks. Over time, this daily check-in with ourselves not only becomes a testament to our resilience and evolution but also a compass, guiding us towards our truest aspirations. In the midst of life's chaos, a consistent journaling habit is our anchor, reminding us of who we are and where we're headed. Use this page to track your daily manifestations.

FOR THE WEEK OF:	Mon	Tue	Wed	Thu	Fri	Sat	Sun
	●	●	●	●	●	●	●
	●	●	●	●	●	●	●
	●	●	●	●	●	●	●
	●	●	●	●	●	●	●
	●	●	●	●	●	●	●
	●	●	●	●	●	●	●
	●	●	●	●	●	●	●
	●	●	●	●	●	●	●
	●	●	●	●	●	●	●
	●	●	●	●	●	●	●
	●	●	●	●	●	●	●
	●	●	●	●	●	●	●
	●	●	●	●	●	●	●

ABOUT THE AUTHOR

Hello,

I'm Joyce Licorish, and I am thrilled to be here with you as the author of this book. I am a creative visionary and the founder of Sweet Inspirations, a YouTube channel that serves as a sanctuary for meaningful daily affirmations, empowering mantras, and inspirational messages. My heart's mission is to spread positivity and wisdom, touching the lives of individuals around the world.

Witnessing the profound influence of affirmations in my own life journey, I am driven to equip others with these empowering tools. As a 6-time Amazon bestselling author, I've seen firsthand how positive mental fortitude can sculpt one's destiny.

Being a parent is among my most cherished roles, fueling my dedication to guiding and championing my children's ambitions. This bond has driven me to urge others to chase their goals relentlessly. It also highlights the universal struggle many face in juggling personal aspirations with familial responsibilities.

Beyond my literary pursuits, I'm an accomplished singer, actor, and voice artist. My passion for artistry knows no bounds, and I'm fiercely dedicated to putting my all into each venture. My endeavors have been recognized both nationally and internationally, including a recent privilege of contributing to a Forbes Panel discussion.

As the CEO of DreamEmpire films, publishing, and voice casting, I embrace my role as a leader and influencer in the creative industry. It brings me great fulfillment to guide and support talented individuals in bringing their dreams to life. However, there are moments in my life where I seemed to hit a plateau that only meditation was able to guide me out of, in addition to this, learning how to properly set my intentions and manifest the life that I want has become an essential part of my daily routine.

Through Sweet Inspirations, I have cultivated a community of like-minded souls who seek inspiration and growth. It is an honor to be part of a platform that spreads love, joy, and positivity to men and women from all walks of life.

As you journey through the pages of this book, I invite you to join me in discovering the transformative power of affirmations and the law of belief. Together, we will unleash the spark of hope and possibility within, embracing our dreams and true potential.

Thank you for being here, and I am excited to embark on this transformative adventure with you. Let's uncover the sweet inspirations that lie within and create a life filled with love, joy, and abundance. **And so it is.**

INTRODUCTION
to: 3 6 9

"If you only knew the magnificence of the 3, 6, and 9, then you would have the key to the universe."

NICOLA TESLA

The 369 Manifestation Method: A Beginner's Guide

The mystique of numbers has fascinated humans for millennia. Among them, the numbers 3, 6, and 9 have captivated imaginations due to their perceived power and symmetry. One person who was particularly entranced by these numbers was the genius inventor, Nikola Tesla. He once stated, "If you only knew the magnificence of the 3, 6, and 9, then you would have the key to the universe."

While Tesla's claim might sound enigmatic, the "And So It Is 369 Method" draws inspiration from his belief in the potency of these numbers. So, how does this method work, and how can a journal assist in your manifestation journey? Let's delve in.

Understanding the 369 Manifestation Method

The method revolves around the idea of channeling energy through repetition and focus. By setting a clear intention and pairing it with positive affirmations, and taking time to let it marinate in your spirit, it's believed that you can align your vibrations with that of the universe, thereby aiding the manifestation process.

Here's a simple breakdown:

3 Start your morning by writing down an affirmation related to your goal **three** times.

6 In the afternoon, revisit and write the same affirmation **six** times, expanding on it.

9 Before bed, write it **nine** times, fully fleshed out letting its message permeate your subconscious as you drift to sleep.

TIP

REMEMBER THE 17 SECOND RULE! Hold the Thought for **17 Seconds** Minimum before moving to the next affirmation.

Understanding the 17-Second Rule

The "17-second rule" is based on the law of attraction, suggesting that like attracts like. The principle is that holding a pure thought for 17 seconds activates a matching vibration, initiating the process of manifestation:

1. Initial 17 seconds: Holding a thought for this duration starts to attract another thought with a similar frequency.

2. 34 seconds: Maintaining that thought for a total of 34 seconds intensifies its vibrational frequency, drawing more similar thoughts.

3. 51 seconds: By 51 seconds, the vibration strengthens even more, increasing the attraction force.

4. 68 seconds: After 68 seconds of uninterrupted focus on a single thought, its power of attraction is significantly amplified, and the process of bringing it into reality begins.

The idea is to maintain focused attention on a particular thought or desire, amplifying its power the longer it's held without distraction. In other words, don't just rattle off a manifestation without lending some thought and heart to it.

The Power of the "And So It Is 369 Journal"

Visualization and emotion are pivotal in the manifestation process. Simply writing things down isn't enough. You need to *feel* the energy of your dreams, visualize them, and fully believe in their imminent reality.

This is where the "And So It Is 369 Journal" comes into play.

By providing you with a dedicated space to structure your daily affirmations, the journal promotes a consistent routine. More than just a book of blank pages, it becomes your manifestation companion, guiding you in scripting your desired future.

Moreover, there's magic in holding a tangible object. Every time you pick up this journal, you're making a commitment to yourself and your dreams. It acts as a daily reminder of your power to shape your destiny.

The Essence of Manifestation

The crux of manifestation lies not just in wanting something but in believing that you can have it. **It's about feeling that joy and gratitude as if your dream has already come to pass.** With clarity in intention and unwavering belief, you can unlock the vast potential of the universe.

Whether you're a seasoned manifester or a curious novice, the 369 Method offers a fresh perspective on the art of bringing dreams to life. And with the aid of the "And So It Is 369 Journal", you're equipped with a powerful tool to help channel those energies. Remember, the universe listens; you just need to know what you're asking for.

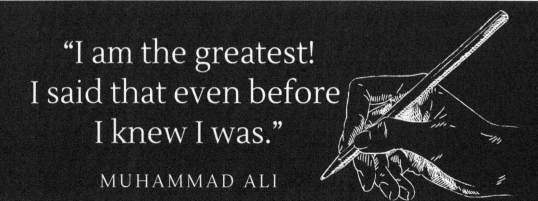

"I am the greatest!
I said that even before
I knew I was."

MUHAMMAD ALI

GRATITUDE
101

"Gratitude makes sense of our past, brings peace for today, and creates a vision for tomorrow."

MELODY BEATTIE

CHAPTER 1: WHY GRATITUDE MATTERS - THE TRANSFORMATIVE POWER OF APPRECIATION

I begin this book with Gratitude and expression of it because without gratitude for what you already have you close yourself off to manifesting what you truly desire. With that in mind, in this chapter, we explore the profound impact of gratitude on our lives and how it holds the key to unlocking a world of positivity, abundance, and joy. Gratitude is more than just a simple expression of thanks; it is a transformative state of being that influences every aspect of our existence.

Gratitude is a lens through which we view the world. When we cultivate an attitude of gratitude, we shift our focus from what is lacking to what we have, from what went wrong to what went right. It enables us to see the blessings and abundance that surround us, even in the midst of challenges.

Practicing gratitude rewires our brain, creating new neural pathways that promote positivity and well-being. Research has shown that grateful individuals experience lower levels of stress, anxiety, and depression while enjoying enhanced emotional resilience and overall life satisfaction.

Gratitude has the power to shift our perspective and transform how we interpret life's events. When we are grateful, we find meaning and lessons in every experience, even the difficult ones. It allows us to grow from adversity and embrace the beauty of life's journey.

Expressing gratitude strengthens our connections with others. When we acknowledge and appreciate those who touch our lives, we deepen our relationships and create a positive ripple effect of kindness and compassion.

Embrace gratitude as a way of life, and watch as it transforms your world from the inside out. Embody the spirit of thankfulness, and you will discover that gratitude truly matters in creating a life of joy, abundance, and fulfillment. **And so it is.**

Write 10 Gratitude Affirmations to express appreciation for the simple things so that you may open yourself up for what you truly desire in your life.

10 Reasons I'm Grateful

1

2

3

4

5

6

7

8

9

10

GRATITUDE AFFIRMATIONS

1. I AM GRATEFUL FOR THE GIFT OF BREATH, AS EACH INHALE AND EXHALE NOURISHES MY BODY AND SOUL WITH LIFE-SUSTAINING ENERGY.

2. I AM THANKFUL FOR THE ABUNDANCE OF NOURISHING FOOD THAT FUELS MY BODY AND PROVIDES ME WITH THE VITALITY TO THRIVE.

3. I AM APPRECIATIVE OF THE PEACEFUL MOMENTS THAT COME WITH SLEEP, REJUVENATING MY MIND AND BODY, ALLOWING ME TO AWAKEN REFRESHED AND RENEWED.

4. I AM GRATEFUL FOR THE ABILITY TO MOVE MY BODY FREELY, EMBRACING THE JOY OF EACH STEP AND THE BLESSINGS OF GOOD HEALTH.

5. I AM THANKFUL FOR THE WONDERS OF NATURE THAT SURROUND ME, OFFERING MOMENTS OF AWE AND INSPIRATION THAT ENRICH MY LIFE.

6. I AM APPRECIATIVE OF THE SIMPLE PLEASURES IN LIFE, LIKE A WARM CUP OF TEA OR THE GENTLE TOUCH OF A LOVED ONE, THAT FILLS MY HEART WITH CONTENTMENT.

7. I AM GRATEFUL FOR THE POWER OF LAUGHTER, AS IT UPLIFTS MY SPIRIT AND CONNECTS ME WITH OTHERS IN MOMENTS OF JOY.

8. I AM THANKFUL FOR THE BEAUTY OF THE SUNRISE AND SUNSET, REMINDING ME OF THE EVER-CHANGING TAPESTRY OF LIFE.

9. I AM APPRECIATIVE OF THE GIFT OF LEARNING AND GROWTH, EMBRACING EACH OPPORTUNITY TO EXPAND MY KNOWLEDGE AND EVOLVE AS AN INDIVIDUAL.

10. I AM GRATEFUL FOR THE LOVE AND SUPPORT OF FAMILY AND FRIENDS, AS THEIR PRESENCE ENRICHES MY LIFE WITH WARMTH AND CONNECTION.

*WITH THESE GRATITUDE AFFIRMATIONS, I EMBRACE THE SIMPLE JOYS THAT LIFE OFFERS AND CULTIVATE A HEART FILLED WITH APPRECIATION FOR THE BLESSINGS THAT SURROUND ME EVERY DAY. **AND SO IT IS.***

I am Grateful

MORNING GRATITUDE

Date: _____

Today I want to feel...

_____

_____

_____

Today I will spread kindness by...

_____

_____

_____

3 things I'm grateful for today are...

_____

_____

_____

"The more you practice
gratitude, the more you see
how much there is to be
grateful for."

DON MIGUEL RUIZ

EVENING GRATITUDE

3 things I'm grateful for today are...

_____

_____

_____

The best part of today was...

_____

_____

_____

What can I learn from today's experiences?

_____

_____

_____

Tomorrow I'm looking forward to...

_____

_____

"Let us be grateful to people
who make us happy; they are the
charming gardeners who make
our souls blossom."

MARCEL PROUST

SELF MASTERY
101

"Your opinion of me is none of my business."

JUDY FORD

CHAPTER 2: THE ONLY OPINION THAT MATTERS ABOUT YOU IS YOURS - MASTERING SELF-PERCEPTION FOR A TRANSFORMED REALITY

In this chapter, we delve into the power of self-perception and how it significantly impacts our reality. Your perception of yourself is the cornerstone of how you experience the world and influences every aspect of your life. Understanding and mastering self-perception can lead to a profound shift in self-talk, empowering you to become the best version of yourself.

Your self-perception shapes your beliefs, thoughts, and actions. If you see yourself as capable, worthy, and deserving, you will approach challenges with confidence and resilience. On the other hand, if your self-perception is tainted with doubt and negativity, you may hold yourself back from reaching your full potential.

It's essential to recognize that the only opinion that truly matters about you is your own. External judgments and opinions may come and go, but your inner dialogue is what shapes your reality. By cultivating a positive self-perception, you can elevate your self-talk and create a better version of yourself.

The first step in shifting self-talk is to become aware of your inner dialogue. Notice the patterns of thought that arise throughout the day. Are they supportive and uplifting, or do they lean towards self-doubt and criticism? Awareness is the key to breaking free from negative self-talk.

Challenge any negative self-perceptions and replace them with empowering affirmations. Acknowledge your strengths, talents, and accomplishments. Celebrate your progress, no matter how small, and recognize that growth is a continuous journey.

FOCUS ON SELF-COMPASSION RATHER THAN SELF-JUDGMENT

Treat yourself with the same kindness and understanding you would offer a close friend. Embrace imperfections as part of being human and allow yourself to learn and grow from mistakes.

Remember that self-perception is not fixed; it can be shaped and transformed through self-awareness and intentional change. Visualize the person you aspire to become and affirm that you are already on the path towards that version of yourself.

Surround yourself with positive influences and people who uplift and support you. The energy you absorb from your environment can significantly impact your self-perception and self-talk.

Practice gratitude for yourself and your journey. Acknowledge your efforts and progress, and express gratitude for your unique qualities and abilities.

Embrace self-love as the foundation of your self-perception. Love and accept yourself unconditionally, just as you are, and cultivate a sense of worthiness and deservingness.

As you master self-perception and shift your self-talk to become a better you, you will witness a transformative shift in your reality. Your newfound positive self-perception will pave the way for greater confidence, resilience, and a deeper connection with your authentic self.

The world responds to how you perceive yourself. When you believe in your worth and potential, the universe aligns with your vision, and doors of opportunity open. Embrace the power of self-perception, and remember that you have the ability to create a reality that reflects the best version of yourself. **And so it is.**

SELF AWARENESS CHECK

Date: _____

What does your ideal "you" look like?

_____

_____

What are your dreams and goals?

_____

_____

What is keeping you from these dreams or goals?

_____

_____

What will it take for you to get out of your own way?

_____

_____

"Oftentimes the biggest obstacle in our path is the shadow we cast upon it. Remember faith and fear cannot reside in the same space! - Take the leap!"

JOYCE LICORISH

SELF-PERCEPTION AFFIRMATIONS

1. I AM WORTHY OF LOVE, SUCCESS, AND ALL THE GOOD LIFE HAS TO OFFER.

2. I BELIEVE IN MY ABILITIES AND TRUST IN MY CAPACITY TO OVERCOME ANY CHALLENGES THAT COME MY WAY.

3. I AM CONFIDENT IN MY DECISIONS, KNOWING THAT I AM GUIDED BY MY INNER WISDOM.

4. I EMBRACE MY UNIQUENESS AND CELEBRATE MY INDIVIDUALITY; I AM A VALUABLE AND IRREPLACEABLE PART OF THIS WORLD.

5. I AM CONSTANTLY GROWING AND EVOLVING, AND I WELCOME THE JOURNEY OF SELF-IMPROVEMENT WITH AN OPEN HEART.

6. I AM DESERVING OF HAPPINESS AND FULFILLMENT, AND I CHOOSE TO CREATE A LIFE THAT BRINGS ME JOY.

7. I AM RESILIENT AND ADAPTABLE; I BOUNCE BACK FROM SETBACKS AND USE THEM AS STEPPING STONES TO SUCCESS.

8. I AM DESERVING OF SELF-COMPASSION AND UNDERSTANDING; I TREAT MYSELF WITH KINDNESS AND GRACE.

9. I AM IN CONTROL OF MY THOUGHTS AND EMOTIONS, AND I CHOOSE TO FOCUS ON THE POSITIVE ASPECTS OF MY LIFE.

10. I AM THE AUTHOR OF MY REALITY; I SHAPE MY EXPERIENCES THROUGH MY THOUGHTS, BELIEFS, AND ACTIONS.

*REPEAT THESE AFFIRMATIONS REGULARLY TO REINFORCE A POSITIVE SELF-PERCEPTION AND CULTIVATE SELF-LOVE AND SELF-EMPOWERMENT. EMBRACE THE BELIEF THAT YOU ARE WORTHY, CAPABLE, AND DESERVING OF A FULFILLING AND SUCCESSFUL LIFE. AS YOU AFFIRM YOUR POSITIVE SELF-PERCEPTION, WATCH HOW YOUR REALITY BEGINS TO ALIGN WITH THE VISION YOU HOLD FOR YOURSELF. YOU HAVE THE POWER TO CREATE A LIFE FILLED WITH LOVE, JOY, AND ABUNDANCE, STARTING FROM WITHIN. **AND SO IT IS.***

I am Worthy!

369 – AND SO IT IS ...

Date:

Morning Manifestation:

1

2

3

☐ *Visualize it for a minimum of 17 Seconds ideally 34 Seconds.*
How does it feel knowing it is yours already?

Afternoon Manifestation:

1

2

3

4

5

6

☐ *Visualize it for 51 Seconds, maintaining focus.*
How does it feel knowing it is yours already?

Night Manifestation:

1

2

3

4

5

6

7

8

9

☐ *Visualize it for 68 Seconds uninterrupted.*
How does it feel knowing it is yours already?

Today's Limitless Possibility:

DAILY PLANNER

S M T W T F S

MOOD:

TODAY'S GOALS

WEATHER:

REMINDER TO:

EXERCISE:

TOTAL MINUTES:	
TOTAL STEPS:	

TODAY'S APPOINTMENT:

TIME	EVENT

THINGS TO GET DONE TODAY:

WATER INTAKE:

MEAL TRACKER:

BREAKFAST:	LUNCH:
DINNER:	SNACKS:

TO CALL OR EMAIL:

MONEY TRACKER:

MONEY IN:	FROM:
MONEY OUT:	FOR:

TODAY I AM GRATEFUL FOR:

NOTES:

FOR TOMORROW:

369 – AND SO IT IS ...

Date:

Morning Manifestation:

1
2
3

☐ *Visualize it for a minimum of 17 Seconds ideally 34 Seconds.*
How does it feel knowing it is yours already?

Afternoon Manifestation:

1
2
3
4
5
6

☐ *Visualize it for 51 Seconds, maintaining focus.*
How does it feel knowing it is yours already?

Night Manifestation:

1
2
3
4
5
6
7
8
9

☐ *Visualize it for 68 Seconds uninterrupted.*
How does it feel knowing it is yours already?

Today's Limitless Possibility:

DAILY PLANNER

MOOD:

TODAY'S GOALS

WEATHER:

REMINDER TO:

EXERCISE:

TOTAL MINUTES	
TOTAL STEPS	

TODAY'S APPOINTMENT:

TIME	EVENT:

THINGS TO GET DONE TODAY:

WATER INTAKE:

MEAL TRACKER:

BREAKFAST:	LUNCH:
DINNER:	SNACKS:

TO CALL OR EMAIL:

MONEY TRACKER:

MONEY IN:	FROM:
MONEY OUT:	FOR:

TODAY I AM GRATEFUL FOR:

NOTES:

FOR TOMORROW:

369 – AND SO IT IS ...

Date: _____

Morning Manifestation:

1 _____
2 _____
3 _____

☐ *Visualize it for a minimum of 17 Seconds ideally 34 Seconds.*
How does it feel knowing it is yours already?

Afternoon Manifestation:

1 _____
2 _____
3 _____
4 _____
5 _____
6 _____

☐ *Visualize it for 51 Seconds, maintaining focus.*
How does it feel knowing it is yours already?

Night Manifestation:

1 _____
2 _____
3 _____
4 _____
5 _____
6 _____
7 _____
8 _____
9 _____

☐ *Visualize it for 68 Seconds uninterrupted.*
How does it feel knowing it is yours already?

Today's Limitless Possibility:

_____
_____

DAILY PLANNER

DATE:

S M T W T F S

MOOD:

TODAY'S GOALS

WEATHER:

REMINDER TO:

EXERCISE:

TOTAL MINUTES:	
TOTAL STEPS:	

TODAY'S APPOINTMENT:

TIME:	EVENT:

THINGS TO GET DONE TODAY:

WATER INTAKE:

MEAL TRACKER:

BREAKFAST:	LUNCH:
DINNER:	SNACKS:

TO CALL OR EMAIL:

MONEY TRACKER:

MONEY IN:	FROM:
MONEY OUT:	FOR:

TODAY I AM GRATEFUL FOR:

NOTES:

FOR TOMORROW:

369 – AND SO IT IS ...

Date:

Morning Manifestation:

1
2
3

☐ Visualize it for a minimum of 17 Seconds ideally 34 Seconds.
How does it feel knowing it is yours already?

Afternoon Manifestation:

1
2
3
4
5
6

☐ Visualize it for 51 Seconds, maintaining focus.
How does it feel knowing it is yours already?

Night Manifestation:

1
2
3
4
5
6
7
8
9

☐ Visualize it for 68 Seconds uninterrupted.
How does it feel knowing it is yours already?

Today's Limitless Possibility:

DAILY PLANNER

S M T W T F S

MOOD:

TODAY'S GOALS

WEATHER:

REMINDER TO:

EXERCISE:

TOTAL MINUTES:	
TOTAL STEPS:	

WATER INTAKE:

○ ○ ○ ○ ○ ○ ○ ○ ○

TODAY'S APPOINTMENT:

TIME:	EVENT

THINGS TO GET DONE TODAY:

_____
_____
_____
_____
_____

MEAL TRACKER:

BREAKFAST:	LUNCH:
DINNER:	SNACKS:

TO CALL OR EMAIL:

_____
_____
_____
_____

MONEY TRACKER:

MONEY IN:	FROM:
MONEY OUT:	FOR:

TODAY I AM GRATEFUL FOR:

_____
_____
_____
_____
_____

NOTES:

_____
_____
_____
_____
_____

FOR TOMORROW:

_____
_____
_____
_____
_____

369 – AND SO IT IS ...

Morning Manifestation:

1
2
3

☐ *Visualize it for a minimum of 17 Seconds ideally 34 Seconds.*
How does it feel knowing it is yours already?

Afternoon Manifestation:

1
2
3
4
5
6

☐ *Visualize it for 51 Seconds, maintaining focus.*
How does it feel knowing it is yours already?

Night Manifestation:

1
2
3
4
5
6
7
8
9

☐ *Visualize it for 68 Seconds uninterrupted.*
How does it feel knowing it is yours already?

Today's Limitless Possibility:

DAILY PLANNER

DATE:

S M T W T F S

MOOD:

TODAY'S GOALS

WEATHER:

REMINDER TO:

EXERCISE:

TOTAL MINUTES:	
TOTAL STEPS:	

TODAY'S APPOINTMENT:

TIME:	EVENT:

THINGS TO GET DONE TODAY:

WATER INTAKE:

MEAL TRACKER:

BREAKFAST:	LUNCH:
DINNER:	SNACKS:

TO CALL OR EMAIL:

MONEY TRACKER:

MONEY IN:	FROM:
MONEY OUT:	FOR:

TODAY I AM GRATEFUL FOR:

NOTES:

FOR TOMORROW:

369 – AND SO IT IS ...

Date:

Morning Manifestation:

1
2
3

☐ Visualize it for a minimum of 17 Seconds ideally 34 Seconds.
How does it feel knowing it is yours already?

Afternoon Manifestation:

1
2
3
4
5
6

☐ Visualize it for 51 Seconds, maintaining focus.
How does it feel knowing it is yours already?

Night Manifestation:

1
2
3
4
5
6
7
8
9

☐ Visualize it for 68 Seconds uninterrupted.
How does it feel knowing it is yours already?

Today's Limitless Possibility:

DAILY PLANNER

S M T W T F S

MOOD:

TODAY'S GOALS

WEATHER:

REMINDER TO:

TODAY'S APPOINTMENT:

TIME	EVENT:

EXERCISE

TOTAL MINUTES	
TOTAL STEPS	

THINGS TO GET DONE TODAY:

WATER INTAKE:

MEAL TRACKER:

BREAKFAST:	LUNCH:
DINNER:	SNACKS:

TO CALL OR EMAIL:

MONEY TRACKER:

MONEY IN:	FROM:
MONEY OUT:	FOR:

TODAY I AM GRATEFUL FOR:

NOTES:

FOR TOMORROW

369 – AND SO IT IS ...

Date: _____

Morning Manifestation:

1 _____
2 _____
3 _____

☐ *Visualize it for a minimum of 17 Seconds ideally 34 Seconds.*
How does it feel knowing it is yours already?

Afternoon Manifestation:

1 _____
2 _____
3 _____
4 _____
5 _____
6 _____

☐ *Visualize it for 51 Seconds, maintaining focus.*
How does it feel knowing it is yours already?

Night Manifestation:

1 _____
2 _____
3 _____
4 _____
5 _____
6 _____
7 _____
8 _____
9 _____

☐ *Visualize it for 68 Seconds uninterrupted.*
How does it feel knowing it is yours already?

Today's Limitless Possibility:

_____

DAILY PLANNER

DATE:

S M T W T F S

MOOD:

TODAY'S GOALS

WEATHER:

REMINDER TO:

EXERCISE:

TOTAL MINUTES:	
TOTAL STEPS:	

WATER INTAKE:

TODAY'S APPOINTMENT:

TIME:	EVENT:

THINGS TO GET DONE TODAY:

MEAL TRACKER:

BREAKFAST:	LUNCH:
DINNER:	SNACKS:

TO CALL OR EMAIL:

MONEY TRACKER:

MONEY IN:	FROM:
MONEY OUT:	FOR:

TODAY I AM GRATEFUL FOR:

NOTES:

FOR TOMORROW:

EMBRACING ABUNDANCE THROUGH AFFIRMATIONS

ASK, AND IT SHALL BE GIVEN TO YOU.

SEEK, AND YE SHALL FIND.

KNOCK, AND IT SHALL BE OPENED UNTO YOU.

MATTHEW 7:7

CHAPTER 3: AFFIRMATIONS FOR ABUNDANCE, HEALTH, WEALTH, HAPPINESS AND FULFILLMENT

Welcome to the transformative world of affirmations, where the power of positive thinking merges with the unlimited potential of the universe. In this chapter, we embark on a journey to manifest abundance, health, wealth, happiness, and fulfillment through the profound practice of affirmations.

Life is a tapestry of possibilities, and our thoughts and beliefs are the threads that weave the fabric of our reality. Affirmations serve as the loom, allowing us to consciously craft our desired outcomes and create a life of richness in all aspects.

As we delve into this chapter, we will explore a tapestry of affirmations that encompass every area of life. Whether it is prosperity, radiant health, inner peace, joyous relationships, or a sense of purpose, we will empower ourselves to manifest the life we truly desire.

Affirmations are not mere wishful thinking; they are potent declarations that reshape our subconscious mind, steering us towards positive action and attracting the experiences we envision. With the law of attraction as our ally, we will learn to align our energy with the universe, magnetizing abundance and prosperity into our lives.

The power of affirmations lies in their ability to change our internal dialogue and perception. As we repeatedly affirm our desires, we create new neural pathways that anchor us in a mindset of possibility and achievement.

THE IMPACT OF AFFIRMATIONS

Throughout this chapter, we will witness the impact of affirmations on different areas of life. From cultivating a strong sense of self-worth to inviting financial abundance, from nurturing our physical and mental well-being to attracting harmonious relationships, we will unlock the keys to a holistic and fulfilling existence.

As you embark on this journey, open your heart and mind to the infinite possibilities that await you. Embrace the transformative energy of affirmations and step into your divine birthright of abundance, health, wealth, happiness, and fulfillment.

May this chapter be a source of inspiration and empowerment, guiding you toward the life that you envision. Together, let us affirm the abundant, joyous, and prosperous reality that we truly deserve. And so it is.

In this section, I give to you a diverse set of affirmations and manifestations for abundance, health, wealth, happiness, love, and fulfillment. Think beyond the basic "I am..." affirmation, and open yourself to limitless possibilities.

Feel free to use these as a starting point and adapt them to resonate with your specific desires and goals.

"Once you make the decision, you will find all the people, resources, and ideas you need every time!"
BOB PROCTOR

ABUNDANCE AFFIRMATIONS

HERE IS A LIST OF 20 ABUNDANCE AFFIRMATIONS:

1. ABUNDANCE FLOWS TO ME EFFORTLESSLY AND ON A DAILY BASIS.
2. I AM OPEN TO RECEIVING ALL THE ABUNDANCE THAT THE UNIVERSE HAS TO OFFER.
3. I ATTRACT PROSPERITY AND ABUNDANCE INTO ALL AREAS OF MY LIFE.
4. MY LIFE IS FILLED WITH LIMITLESS OPPORTUNITIES FOR GROWTH AND SUCCESS.
5. I AM A MAGNET FOR FINANCIAL ABUNDANCE AND MATERIAL WEALTH.
6. THE UNIVERSE SUPPORTS AND REWARDS MY POSITIVE ACTIONS WITH ABUNDANCE.
7. I AM GRATEFUL FOR THE ABUNDANCE THAT SURROUNDS ME EVERY DAY.
8. ABUNDANCE IS MY BIRTHRIGHT, AND I CLAIM IT NOW WITH CONFIDENCE.
9. MONEY COMES TO ME EASILY AND EFFORTLESSLY FROM MULTIPLE SOURCES.
10. I ATTRACT PROSPERITY BY STAYING ALIGNED WITH MY TRUE PURPOSE.
11. ABUNDANCE FLOWS FREELY THROUGH ME AND MANIFESTS IN ALL AREAS OF MY LIFE.
12. EVERY DAY, I AM ATTRACTING MORE WEALTH, SUCCESS, AND PROSPERITY INTO MY LIFE.
13. I AM DESERVING OF ABUNDANCE, AND THE UNIVERSE ALWAYS PROVIDES FOR ME.
14. WITH EVERY BREATH I TAKE, I AM BECOMING MORE ALIGNED WITH THE ENERGY OF ABUNDANCE.
15. I AM A MAGNET FOR PROSPERITY, AND I ATTRACT WEALTH EFFORTLESSLY.
16. MY POTENTIAL TO SUCCEED IS LIMITLESS, AND ABUNDANCE IS A NATURAL PART OF MY LIFE.
17. I GRATEFULLY RECEIVE ALL THE WEALTH AND PROSPERITY THAT THE UNIVERSE SHOWERS UPON ME.
18. I AM OPEN TO ABUNDANCE IN ITS MANY FORMS, WHETHER IT BE HEALTH, WEALTH, LOVE, OR HAPPINESS.
19. I AM CONSTANTLY SURROUNDED BY ABUNDANCE, AND IT FEELS SO GOOD TO BE PROSPEROUS.
20. ABUNDANCE IS MY BIRTHRIGHT, AND I CLAIM IT NOW WITH GRATITUDE AND JOY.

UTILIZING THESE AFFIRMATIONS AS DAILY REMINDERS CAN HELP TO NURTURE A MINDSET OF PROSPERITY AND ATTRACT ABUNDANCE INTO YOUR LIFE. **AND SO IT IS!**

I am Abundant!

369 – AND SO IT IS ...

Date:

Morning Manifestation:

1
2
3

☐ *Visualize it for a minimum of 17 Seconds ideally 34 Seconds.*
How does it feel knowing it is yours already?

Afternoon Manifestation:

1
2
3
4
5
6

☐ *Visualize it for 51 Seconds, maintaining focus.*
How does it feel knowing it is yours already?

Night Manifestation:

1
2
3
4
5
6
7
8
9

☐ *Visualize it for 68 Seconds uninterrupted.*
How does it feel knowing it is yours already?

Today's Limitless Possibility:

DAILY PLANNER

S M T W T F S

MOOD:

TODAY'S GOALS

WEATHER:

REMINDER TO

EXERCISE:

TOTAL MINUTES:	
TOTAL STEPS:	

TODAY'S APPOINTMENT:

TIME	EVENT:

THINGS TO GET DONE TODAY:

WATER INTAKE:

MEAL TRACKER:

BREAKFAST:	LUNCH:
DINNER:	SNACKS:

TO CALL OR EMAIL:

MONEY TRACKER:

MONEY IN:	FROM:
MONEY OUT:	FOR:

TODAY I AM GRATEFUL FOR:

NOTES:

FOR TOMORROW:

HEALTH AFFIRMATIONS

THE PATH TO RADIANT HEALTH

YOUR HEALTH IS A REFLECTION OF THE DAILY CHOICES YOU MAKE AND THE BELIEFS YOU HOLD ABOUT YOURSELF. BY EMBRACING POSITIVE AFFIRMATIONS, YOU CAN CHOOSE TO CONSCIOUSLY ALIGN YOUR MINDSET WITH WELL-BEING AND VITALITY, OPENING THE DOOR FOR THE BODY TO FOLLOW.

HERE ARE 10 HEALTH AFFIRMATIONS TO GUIDE YOU ON YOUR JOURNEY TO OPTIMAL HEALTH:

1. MY BODY IS VIBRANT AND FULL OF ENERGY, RADIATING WITH GOOD HEALTH.
2. I AM IN PERFECT HARMONY WITH THE NATURAL RHYTHMS OF MY BODY AND MIND.
3. I MAKE HEALTHY CHOICES THAT NOURISH MY BODY AND MIND.
4. EVERY DAY, I BECOME HEALTHIER AND STRONGER.
5. I AM FREE OF ALL ILLNESS AND DISEASE; MY BODY IS A TEMPLE OF HEALTH.
6. I LOVE AND ACCEPT MY BODY UNCONDITIONALLY, JUST AS IT IS.
7. MY IMMUNE SYSTEM IS STRONG, PROTECTING ME FROM ANY HARM.
8. I RELEASE ANY TENSION OR STRESS FROM MY BODY, AND I EMBRACE RELAXATION AND WELL-BEING.
9. I AM THE MASTER OF MY HEALTH, AND I TAKE RESPONSIBILITY FOR MY WELL-BEING.
10. I RADIATE HEALTH AND VITALITY, INSPIRING OTHERS TO DO THE SAME.

INCORPORATE THESE AFFIRMATIONS INTO YOUR DAILY ROUTINE AND WATCH AS THEY MANIFEST INTO PHYSICAL WELL-BEING. REMEMBER, A HARMONIOUS MINDSET PAVES THE WAY FOR A HARMONIOUS BODY. EMBRACE THESE AFFIRMATIONS WITH BELIEF, AND LET THEM GUIDE YOU ON YOUR PATH TO RADIANT HEALTH AND VITALITY.
AND SO IT IS!

I am Healthy.

369 – AND SO IT IS ...

Date: _____

Morning Manifestation:

1 _____
2 _____
3 _____

☐ *Visualize it for a minimum of 17 Seconds ideally 34 Seconds.*
How does it feel knowing it is yours already?

Afternoon Manifestation:

1 _____
2 _____
3 _____
4 _____
5 _____
6 _____

☐ *Visualize it for 51 Seconds, maintaining focus.*
How does it feel knowing it is yours already?

Night Manifestation:

1 _____
2 _____
3 _____
4 _____
5 _____
6 _____
7 _____
8 _____
9 _____

☐ *Visualize it for 68 Seconds uninterrupted.*
How does it feel knowing it is yours already?

Today's Limitless Possibility:

_____

_____

DAILY PLANNER

DATE:

(S) (M) (T) (W) (T) (F) (S)

MOOD:

TODAY'S GOALS

WEATHER:

REMINDER TO:

TODAY'S APPOINTMENT

TIME	EVENT

EXERCISE:

THINGS TO GET DONE TODAY:

TOTAL MINUTES	
TOTAL STEPS	

WATER INTAKE:

MEAL TRACKER:

TO CALL OR EMAIL

MONEY TRACKER:

BREAKFAST	LUNCH
DINNER	SNACKS

MONEY IN	FROM
MONEY OUT	FOR

TODAY I AM GRATEFUL FOR:

NOTES:

FOR TOMORROW:

369 – AND SO IT IS ...

Date: _____

Morning Manifestation:

1 _____
2 _____
3 _____

☐ *Visualize it for a minimum of 17 Seconds ideally 34 Seconds.*
How does it feel knowing it is yours already?

Afternoon Manifestation:

1 _____
2 _____
3 _____
4 _____
5 _____
6 _____

☐ *Visualize it for 51 Seconds, maintaining focus.*
How does it feel knowing it is yours already?

Night Manifestation:

1 _____
2 _____
3 _____
4 _____
5 _____
6 _____
7 _____
8 _____
9 _____

☐ *Visualize it for 68 Seconds uninterrupted.*
How does it feel knowing it is yours already?

Today's Limitless Possibility:

_____
_____

WEALTH AFFIRMATIONS

THE JOURNEY TO FINANCIAL PROSPERITY

TRUE WEALTH ISN'T JUST ABOUT MONETARY GAIN. IT'S ABOUT CULTIVATING A MINDSET THAT EMBRACES ABUNDANCE, GRATITUDE, AND THE ENDLESS OPPORTUNITIES THE UNIVERSE OFFERS. WHEN WE SHIFT OUR THOUGHTS TOWARDS PROSPERITY AND OPEN OUR HEARTS TO RECEIVING, WE ALIGN WITH THE ENERGY OF ABUNDANCE. ALLOW THESE 10 AFFIRMATIONS TO GUIDE YOU ON YOUR PATH TO FINANCIAL SUCCESS:

1. I AM A MONEY MAGNET; ABUNDANCE FLOWS TO ME FROM ALL DIRECTIONS.
2. WEALTH AND SUCCESS ARE MY NATURAL STATE OF BEING.
3. I AM WORTHY OF RECEIVING IMMENSE WEALTH AND FINANCIAL PROSPERITY.
4. I ATTRACT LUCRATIVE OPPORTUNITIES THAT LEAD TO GREAT FINANCIAL ABUNDANCE.
5. MY BANK ACCOUNT IS ALWAYS INCREASING, AND I MANAGE MY MONEY WISELY.
6. I CREATE MULTIPLE STREAMS OF INCOME EFFORTLESSLY.
7. I AM FINANCIALLY INDEPENDENT AND FREE TO PURSUE MY PASSIONS.
8. WEALTH AND SUCCESS COME TO ME EASILY, AND I AM GRATEFUL FOR THEM.
9. I USE MY WEALTH TO CREATE POSITIVE CHANGE AND IMPACT IN THE WORLD.
10. I AM OPEN TO RECEIVING WEALTH AND ABUNDANCE IN SURPRISING AND UNEXPECTED WAYS.

REMEMBER, WEALTH IS NOT SOLELY ABOUT ACCUMULATION BUT ALSO ABOUT THE FREEDOM, PEACE, AND OPPORTUNITIES IT CAN OFFER. AFFIRM YOUR JOURNEY WITH BELIEF, KNOWING THAT THE UNIVERSE SUPPORTS YOUR VISION OF PROSPERITY. **AND SO IT IS.**

I am Wealthy.

369 – AND SO IT IS ...

Date: _____

Morning Manifestation:

1 _____
2 _____
3 _____

☐ *Visualize it for a minimum of 17 Seconds ideally 34 Seconds.*
How does it feel knowing it is yours already?

Afternoon Manifestation:

1 _____
2 _____
3 _____
4 _____
5 _____
6 _____

☐ *Visualize it for 51 Seconds, maintaining focus.*
How does it feel knowing it is yours already?

Night Manifestation:

1 _____
2 _____
3 _____
4 _____
5 _____
6 _____
7 _____
8 _____
9 _____

☐ *Visualize it for 68 Seconds uninterrupted.*
How does it feel knowing it is yours already?

Today's Limitless Possibility:

_____
_____

DAILY PLANNER

DATE:

MOOD:

TODAY'S GOALS

WEATHER:

REMINDER TO:

EXERCISE

TOTAL MINUTES:	
TOTAL STEPS:	

TODAY'S APPOINTMENT:

TIME	EVENT

THINGS TO GET DONE TODAY:

WATER INTAKE:

MEAL TRACKER:

BREAKFAST:	LUNCH:
DINNER:	SNACKS:

TO CALL OR EMAIL:

MONEY TRACKER:

MONEY IN:	FROM:
MONEY OUT:	FOR:

TODAY I AM GRATEFUL FOR:

NOTES:

FOR TOMORROW:

LOVE AFFIRMATIONS

EMBARKING ON A JOURNEY OF LOVE

LOVE IS NOT JUST A FEELING BUT A STATE OF BEING, A CONSCIOUS CHOICE TO LIVE WITH OPEN-HEARTEDNESS AND VULNERABILITY. AT ITS CORE, LOVE IS THE MOST PROFOUND CONNECTION WE CAN EXPERIENCE, UNITING OUR SOULS WITH THE WORLD AROUND US. AS YOU STEP INTO THIS REALM OF BOUNDLESS LOVE, LET THESE 10 AFFIRMATIONS GUIDE YOUR HEART AND ILLUMINATE YOUR PATH:

1. I AM WORTHY OF LOVE, AND I ATTRACT LOVING AND SUPPORTIVE RELATIONSHIPS.
2. LOVE FLOWS TO ME EFFORTLESSLY, AND I AM OPEN TO GIVING AND RECEIVING LOVE.
3. I AM SURROUNDED BY PEOPLE WHO LOVE AND APPRECIATE ME FOR WHO I AM.
4. MY HEART IS OPEN, AND I ATTRACT A LOVING AND FULFILLING ROMANTIC PARTNER.
5. I AM A MAGNET FOR HEALTHY AND NURTURING FRIENDSHIPS.
6. I LOVE AND ACCEPT MYSELF COMPLETELY, WHICH ALLOWS OTHERS TO LOVE ME TOO.
7. LOVE IS THE FOUNDATION OF ALL MY RELATIONSHIPS, BRINGING HARMONY AND JOY.
8. I RELEASE ANY PAST HURTS AND OPEN MYSELF TO EXPERIENCING LOVE AGAIN.
9. I AM A SOURCE OF LOVE AND COMPASSION, SHARING IT WITH THE WORLD.
10. LOVE IS ABUNDANT IN MY LIFE, AND I AM GRATEFUL FOR THE LOVE I RECEIVE.

REMEMBER, THE LOVE YOU SEEK IS ALSO SEEKING YOU. WITH AN OPEN HEART, YOU CAN MANIFEST AND ATTRACT THE LOVE THAT RESONATES WITH YOUR ESSENCE, FILLING YOUR LIFE WITH WARMTH, UNDERSTANDING, AND CONNECTION. EMBRACE LOVE IN ITS MANY FORMS AND LET IT TRANSFORM YOUR EXISTENCE. AND SO IT IS.

I attract the Love I deserve!

369 – AND SO IT IS ...

Date:

Morning Manifestation:

1
2
3

☐ *Visualize it for a minimum of 17 Seconds ideally 34 Seconds.*
How does it feel knowing it is yours already?

Afternoon Manifestation:

1
2
3
4
5
6

☐ *Visualize it for 51 Seconds, maintaining focus.*
How does it feel knowing it is yours already?

Night Manifestation:

1
2
3
4
5
6
7
8
9

☐ *Visualize it for 68 Seconds uninterrupted.*
How does it feel knowing it is yours already?

Today's Limitless Possibility:

DAILY PLANNER

S M T W T F S

MOOD:

TODAY'S GOALS

WEATHER:

REMINDER TO:

TODAY'S APPOINTMENT:

TIME:	EVENT:

EXERCISE:

TOTAL MINUTES:	
TOTAL STEPS:	

THINGS TO GET DONE TODAY:

WATER INTAKE:

MEAL TRACKER:

BREAKFAST:	LUNCH:
DINNER:	SNACKS:

TO CALL OR EMAIL:

MONEY TRACKER:

MONEY IN:	FROM:
MONEY OUT:	FOR:

TODAY I AM GRATEFUL FOR:

NOTES:

FOR TOMORROW:

FULFILLMENT AFFIRMATIONS

THE QUEST FOR INNER FULFILLMENT

FULFILLMENT ISN'T SOLELY ABOUT ACHIEVING OUR DREAMS OR REACHING MILESTONES. IT'S ABOUT THE JOURNEY, THE LESSONS WE LEARN, AND THE DEEP CONTENTMENT WE FIND ALONG THE WAY. TRUE FULFILLMENT COMES FROM ALIGNING WITH OUR CORE VALUES, PASSIONS, AND PURPOSES, REALIZING THAT EVERY EXPERIENCE ADDS TO OUR UNIQUE TAPESTRY OF LIFE. ALLOW THESE 10 AFFIRMATIONS TO INSPIRE AND REMIND YOU OF THE BEAUTY OF LIVING A FULFILLING LIFE:

1. I LIVE A LIFE FILLED WITH PURPOSE AND MEANING, FINDING FULFILLMENT IN EVERY MOMENT.
2. I AM ALIGNED WITH MY PASSIONS, AND THEY LEAD ME TO FULFILLMENT AND SUCCESS.
3. I EMBRACE CHALLENGES AS OPPORTUNITIES FOR GROWTH AND FULFILLMENT.
4. MY LIFE'S JOURNEY IS FULL OF FULFILLMENT, AND I CELEBRATE EACH STEP.
5. I AM LIVING MY DREAMS AND ASPIRATIONS, FULLY SATISFIED WITH MY PATH.
6. MY WORK IS A SOURCE OF FULFILLMENT, ALLOWING ME TO MAKE A POSITIVE IMPACT.
7. I TRUST THAT THE UNIVERSE GUIDES ME TOWARD GREATER FULFILLMENT AND PURPOSE.
8. I AM CONTENT WITH WHAT I HAVE WHILE CONTINUOUSLY WORKING TOWARDS MY GOALS.
9. MY LIFE IS FILLED WITH JOY AND CONTENTMENT, AND I SHARE IT WITH OTHERS.
10. I AM FULFILLED IN ALL ASPECTS OF LIFE, APPRECIATING THE ABUNDANCE AROUND ME.

FULFILLMENT IS A HARMONIOUS BLEND OF INNER PEACE, AMBITION, AND GRATITUDE. BY CHERISHING EVERY MOMENT AND RECOGNIZING THE PROFOUNDNESS IN OUR DAILY LIVES, WE CAN UNLOCK UNPARALLELED CONTENTMENT AND JOY. DIVE DEEP INTO THE ESSENCE OF FULFILLMENT, AND LET IT RESONATE WITH EVERY HEARTBEAT. **AND SO IT IS.**

I live a fulfilled life.

369 – AND SO IT IS ...

Date: _____

Morning Manifestation:

1 _____
2 _____
3 _____

☐ *Visualize it for a minimum of 17 Seconds ideally 34 Seconds.*
How does it feel knowing it is yours already?

Afternoon Manifestation:

1 _____
2 _____
3 _____
4 _____
5 _____
6 _____

☐ *Visualize it for 51 Seconds, maintaining focus.*
How does it feel knowing it is yours already?

Night Manifestation:

1 _____
2 _____
3 _____
4 _____
5 _____
6 _____
7 _____
8 _____
9 _____

☐ *Visualize it for 68 Seconds uninterrupted.*
How does it feel knowing it is yours already?

Today's Limitless Possibility:

_____
_____

DAILY PLANNER

(S) (M) (T) (W) (T) (F) (S)

MOOD:

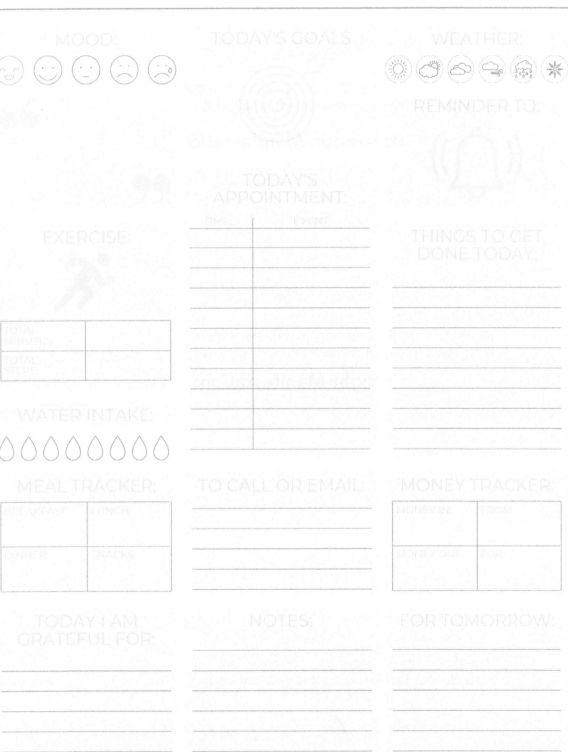

TODAY'S GOALS

WEATHER:

REMINDER TO:

EXERCISE:

| TOTAL MINUTES | |
| TOTAL STEPS | |

TODAY'S APPOINTMENT:

TIME	EVENT

THINGS TO GET DONE TODAY:

WATER INTAKE:

MEAL TRACKER:

BREAKFAST	LUNCH
DINNER	SNACKS

TO CALL OR EMAIL

MONEY TRACKER:

MONEY IN	FROM
MONEY OUT	FOR

TODAY I AM GRATEFUL FOR:

NOTES:

FOR TOMORROW:

369 – AND SO IT IS ...

Morning Manifestation:

1 _____
2 _____
3 _____

[ ] *Visualize it for a minimum of 17 Seconds ideally 34 Seconds.*
How does it feel knowing it is yours already?

Afternoon Manifestation:

1 _____
2 _____
3 _____
4 _____
5 _____
6 _____

[ ] *Visualize it for 51 Seconds, maintaining focus.*
How does it feel knowing it is yours already?

Night Manifestation:

1 _____
2 _____
3 _____
4 _____
5 _____
6 _____
7 _____
8 _____
9 _____

[ ] *Visualize it for 68 Seconds uninterrupted.*
How does it feel knowing it is yours already?

Today's Limitless Possibility:

_____

DAILY PLANNER

DATE:

S M T W T F S

MOOD:

TODAY'S GOALS

WEATHER:

REMINDER TO:

TODAY'S
APPOINTMENT:

TIME	EVENT

EXERCISE:

THINGS TO GET
DONE TODAY:

TOTAL MINUTES	
TOTAL STEPS	

WATER INTAKE:

MEAL TRACKER:

TO CALL OR EMAIL

MONEY TRACKER:

BREAKFAST	LUNCH
DINNER	SNACKS

MONEY IN	FROM
MONEY OUT	FOR

TODAY I AM
GRATEFUL FOR:

NOTES:

FOR TOMORROW:

369 – AND SO IT IS ...

Date: _____

Morning Manifestation:

1 _____
2 _____
3 _____

☐ *Visualize it for a minimum of 17 Seconds ideally 34 Seconds.*
How does it feel knowing it is yours already?

Afternoon Manifestation:

1 _____
2 _____
3 _____
4 _____
5 _____
6 _____

☐ *Visualize it for 51 Seconds, maintaining focus.*
How does it feel knowing it is yours already?

Night Manifestation:

1 _____
2 _____
3 _____
4 _____
5 _____
6 _____
7 _____
8 _____
9 _____

☐ *Visualize it for 68 Seconds uninterrupted.*
How does it feel knowing it is yours already?

Today's Limitless Possibility:

_____
_____

DAILY PLANNER

DATE:

S M T W T F S

MOOD:

TODAY'S GOALS

WEATHER:

REMINDER TO:

EXERCISE:

TODAY'S APPOINTMENT:

TIME	EVENT

THINGS TO GET DONE TODAY:

TOTAL MINUTES:	
TOTAL STEPS:	

WATER INTAKE:

MEAL TRACKER:

BREAKFAST	LUNCH
DINNER	SNACKS

TO CALL OR EMAIL

MONEY TRACKER:

MONEY IN	FROM
MONEY OUT	FOR

TODAY I AM GRATEFUL FOR:

NOTES:

FOR TOMORROW:

MANIFESTING 101

"The world is a mirror forever reflecting what you are doing within yourself."

NEVILLE GODDARD

THE KEY TO SUCCESSFUL MANIFESTATION

Remember, the key to successful manifestation is to repeat these affirmations consistently, genuinely believe in them, and take aligned actions toward your goals. This is work, this is the work of aligning yourself with your intentions and with your intended path forward. Each person's journey is unique, so adapt these manifestations to suit your own desires and aspirations. Manifestations work best when they come from the heart and resonate with your deepest desires. May you attract all the abundance, health, wealth, happiness, love, and fulfillment that you seek in your life! Manifesting your desires into reality is a blend of mental, emotional, and practical processes. While there's no guaranteed formula, many experts and proponents of manifestation techniques believe in the following steps to make your dreams come true:

1. Clarity of Intention: Be crystal clear about what you want. Vague or ambiguous goals aren't as effective. For example, instead of saying, "I want to be rich," try "I want to earn $100,000 by the end of next year."

2. Visualization: Take a moment each day to close your eyes and vividly imagine having what you desire. Picture every detail, the emotions you'd feel, the people you'd be with, and the environment around you.

3. Positive Affirmations: Develop positive statements that affirm your desired outcome. Repeat them daily, allowing them to sink into your subconscious.

4. Emotional Alignment: Feel the emotions that achieving your goal would bring. Whether it's joy, satisfaction, pride, or love, let these feelings permeate your daily life.

5. Gratitude: Cultivate a genuine sense of gratitude for what you already have and for what's coming your way. Trust that the universe is working in your favor.

6. Action: While mindset is crucial, so is taking the necessary steps toward your goal. Take inspired action related to your desire.

7. Letting Go: Once you've done your part, release your attachment to the outcome. Trust that what's meant for you will come to you.

8. Stay Open to Signs: Often, the universe sends us signs or nudges us in the right direction. Stay observant.

9. Limit Negative Influences: Surround yourself with positivity and avoid naysayers or energies that might dampen your enthusiasm.

10. Patience and Persistence: Understand that good things may take time. Stay patient and persistent. Continue your practices even if you don't see immediate results.

11. Self-belief: Trust in yourself and your capability to achieve your desires. Believe that you are deserving of your dreams.

12. Educate Yourself: Read books, attend workshops, or join groups that align with your goals. Knowledge can act as a catalyst for manifestation.

13. Journaling: Keep a journal to track your feelings, progress, and any signs you receive. It helps in understanding patterns and boosting motivation.

Lastly, remember that manifestation is as much about the journey as the destination. It's an opportunity to understand yourself better, to grow, and to learn. Embrace the entire process, and trust that the universe is conspiring in your favor.

"You cannot attract what you are not, so become the very thing that you wish for and watch God open doors no man can close!"

JOYCE LICORISH

CHAPTER 4 TRANSCENDING "I AM"... EMBRACE THE POWER OF DIVERSE AFFIRMATIONS

You've journeyed through the realm of "I Am" affirmations, and now it's time to take a quantum leap into the wondrous world of diverse affirmations. As you already know, affirmations are transformative statements that hold the key to shifting your mindset, beliefs, and emotions toward a more positive and empowering direction. While "I am" affirmations are widely recognized and effective, there exists a vast array of other affirmations that can elevate every facet of your life. Join us on this journey as we explore the boundless potential of various affirmation types and unlock the secrets to a more abundant, fulfilling, and joyful existence.

I attract ...
I can ...
I will ...
I believe ...
I choose ...
I deserve ...
I release ...
I embrace ...
I am becoming ...

Why not branch out and try more than just the basic I am affirmations?

I HAVE

Affirming that you already possess what you desire can help reinforce feelings of abundance and gratitude.
- *Example: "I have all the resources I need to achieve my goals."*

I ATTRACT

This type of affirmation focuses on drawing positive experiences and opportunities into your life.
- *Example: "I attract success and prosperity in all areas of my life."*

I CAN

Encouraging self-belief and confidence, "I can" affirmations help you overcome self-doubt and limitations.
- Example: "I can overcome any challenge that comes my way."

I WILL

These affirmations express determination and commitment to future actions and outcomes.
- Example: "I will make choices that align with my highest good."

I CHOOSE

By affirming your choices, you take ownership of your decisions and empower yourself to create the life you want.
- Example: "I choose to focus on the positive aspects of every situation."

I DESERVE

Affirming your worthiness and deservingness can help you attract what you genuinely believe you should have.
- Example: "I deserve love, happiness, and all the good that life has to offer."

I EMBRACE

These affirmations invite you to embrace and allow in new experiences, growth, and positive change.

- Example: "I embrace change and welcome new opportunities with an open heart."

I RELEASE

Letting go of negative emotions or limiting beliefs can be facilitated through "I release" affirmations.

- Example: "I release all fear and doubt, allowing space for confidence and courage."

I TRUST

Trusting in yourself and the universe can help reduce anxiety and foster a sense of inner peace.

- Example: "I trust that everything happens for my highest good."

I AM BECOMING

These affirmations acknowledge your growth and progress, emphasizing that positive change is an ongoing process.

- Example: "I am becoming stronger, wiser, and more resilient every day."

Remember that the effectiveness of affirmations lies in repetition and emotional connection. Choose affirmations that resonate deeply with you and your goals, and incorporate them into your daily routine. Over time, they can help rewire your thought patterns and support your journey toward a more positive and fulfilling life.

I HAVE
AFFIRMATIONS

HERE ARE TEN "I HAVE" AFFIRMATIONS TO AFFIRM LOVE, A HAPPY FAMILY, ABUNDANCE, FAITH, SECURITY, HOPE, AND A BRIGHT FUTURE AHEAD:

1. I HAVE BOUNDLESS LOVE WITHIN ME, AND I ATTRACT LOVING RELATIONSHIPS INTO MY LIFE EFFORTLESSLY.
2. I HAVE A HAPPY AND HARMONIOUS FAMILY, AND OUR CONNECTIONS DEEPEN WITH EACH PASSING DAY.
3. I HAVE AN ABUNDANCE MINDSET, AND PROSPERITY FLOWS ABUNDANTLY INTO ALL AREAS OF MY LIFE.
4. I HAVE UNWAVERING FAITH IN MYSELF AND THE UNIVERSE, KNOWING THAT EVERYTHING UNFOLDS PERFECTLY.
5. I HAVE A STRONG SENSE OF SECURITY AND TRUST THAT I AM ALWAYS SAFE AND PROTECTED.
6. I HAVE UNWAVERING HOPE FOR THE FUTURE, AND I EMBRACE LIFE'S CHALLENGES WITH OPTIMISM.
7. I HAVE A BRIGHT AND PROMISING FUTURE AHEAD, FILLED WITH ENDLESS OPPORTUNITIES AND POSSIBILITIES.
8. I HAVE A HEART FULL OF GRATITUDE, AND I APPRECIATE ALL THE BLESSINGS THAT SURROUND ME.
9. I HAVE THE POWER TO CREATE POSITIVE CHANGE IN MY LIFE AND THE LIVES OF OTHERS.
10. I HAVE A CLEAR VISION OF MY DREAMS AND GOALS, AND I AM MOVING TOWARDS THEM WITH UNWAVERING DETERMINATION.

RECITE THESE AFFIRMATIONS DAILY, AND LET THEM SINK DEEP INTO YOUR CONSCIOUSNESS. FEEL THE EMOTIONS ASSOCIATED WITH EACH AFFIRMATION AS YOU SAY THEM, AND WATCH AS THEY POSITIVELY INFLUENCE YOUR THOUGHTS, ACTIONS, AND EXPERIENCES. THE POWER OF AFFIRMATIONS LIES IN THEIR ABILITY TO SHAPE YOUR BELIEFS AND TRANSFORM YOUR REALITY. EMBRACE THESE AFFIRMATIONS WITH OPENNESS AND TRUST, AND WITNESS THE MAGIC THEY CAN BRING INTO YOUR LIFE.
AND SO IT IS!

I have a beautiful life.

369 – AND SO IT IS ...

Morning Manifestation:

1
2
3

☐ Visualize it for a minimum of 17 Seconds ideally 34 Seconds.
How does it feel knowing it is yours already?

Afternoon Manifestation:

1
2
3
4
5
6

☐ Visualize it for 51 Seconds, maintaining focus.
How does it feel knowing it is yours already?

Night Manifestation:

1
2
3
4
5
6
7
8
9

☐ Visualize it for 68 Seconds uninterrupted.
How does it feel knowing it is yours already?

Today's Limitless Possibility:

DAILY PLANNER

S M T W T F S

MOOD:

TODAY'S GOALS

WEATHER:

REMINDER TO:

EXERCISE:

| TOTAL MINUTES: | |
| TOTAL STEPS: | |

TODAY'S APPOINTMENT:

TIME:	EVENT:

THINGS TO GET DONE TODAY:

WATER INTAKE:

MEAL TRACKER:

BREAKFAST:	LUNCH:
DINNER:	SNACKS:

TO CALL OR EMAIL:

MONEY TRACKER:

MONEY IN:	FROM:
MONEY OUT:	FOR:

TODAY I AM GRATEFUL FOR:

NOTES:

FOR TOMORROW:

I ATTRACT AFFIRMATIONS

HERE ARE TEN "I ATTRACT" AFFIRMATIONS TO MANIFEST JOY, LOVE, AND ABUNDANCE INTO YOUR LIFE:

1. I ATTRACT BOUNDLESS JOY INTO MY LIFE, AND I FIND HAPPINESS IN EVEN THE SIMPLEST OF MOMENTS.
2. I ATTRACT LOVE EFFORTLESSLY; MY HEART IS OPEN, AND I AM READY TO GIVE AND RECEIVE LOVE IN ABUNDANCE.
3. I ATTRACT LOVING AND SUPPORTIVE RELATIONSHIPS THAT UPLIFT AND INSPIRE ME ON MY JOURNEY.
4. I ATTRACT FINANCIAL ABUNDANCE AND PROSPERITY FROM MULTIPLE SOURCES, CREATING A LIFE OF FREEDOM AND OPPORTUNITY.
5. I ATTRACT OPPORTUNITIES FOR GROWTH AND SUCCESS, AND I EMBRACE THEM WITH ENTHUSIASM AND CONFIDENCE.
6. I ATTRACT POSITIVE ENERGY AND REPEL ALL NEGATIVITY; MY LIFE IS FILLED WITH HARMONIOUS EXPERIENCES.
7. I ATTRACT ABUNDANCE IN ALL FORMS, AND I GRATEFULLY RECEIVE THE GIFTS THAT THE UNIVERSE BESTOWS UPON ME.
8. I ATTRACT OPPORTUNITIES TO SERVE AND MAKE A DIFFERENCE, SHARING MY UNIQUE GIFTS WITH THE WORLD.
9. I ATTRACT VIBRANT HEALTH AND WELL-BEING; MY BODY AND MIND ARE IN PERFECT HARMONY.
10. I ATTRACT A LIFE OF PURPOSE AND FULFILLMENT, ALIGNING WITH MY TRUE PASSIONS AND DESIRES.

REPEAT THESE AFFIRMATIONS REGULARLY WITH CONVICTION AND BELIEF. VISUALIZE YOURSELF ALREADY EXPERIENCING THE JOY, LOVE, AND ABUNDANCE THEY DESCRIBE. AS YOU FOCUS ON THESE POSITIVE ENERGIES, YOU'LL BEGIN TO NOTICE A SHIFT IN YOUR REALITY AS YOU ATTRACT MORE OF WHAT YOU DESIRE INTO YOUR LIFE. REMEMBER, THE KEY IS TO EMBODY THE EMOTIONS ASSOCIATED WITH THESE AFFIRMATIONS AND TAKE INSPIRED ACTIONS TOWARD YOUR GOALS. TRUST IN THE PROCESS, AND LET THE UNIVERSE BRING YOU THE JOY, LOVE, AND ABUNDANCE YOU DESERVE. **AND SO IT IS!**

I attract amazing opportunities!

369 – AND SO IT IS ...

Date: _____

Morning Manifestation:

1 _____
2 _____
3 _____

☐ *Visualize it for a minimum of 17 Seconds ideally 34 Seconds.*
How does it feel knowing it is yours already?

Afternoon Manifestation:

1 _____
2 _____
3 _____
4 _____
5 _____
6 _____

☐ *Visualize it for 51 Seconds, maintaining focus.*
How does it feel knowing it is yours already?

Night Manifestation:

1 _____
2 _____
3 _____
4 _____
5 _____
6 _____
7 _____
8 _____
9 _____

☐ *Visualize it for 68 Seconds uninterrupted.*
How does it feel knowing it is yours already?

Today's Limitless Possibility:

_____
_____

DAILY PLANNER

S M T W T F S

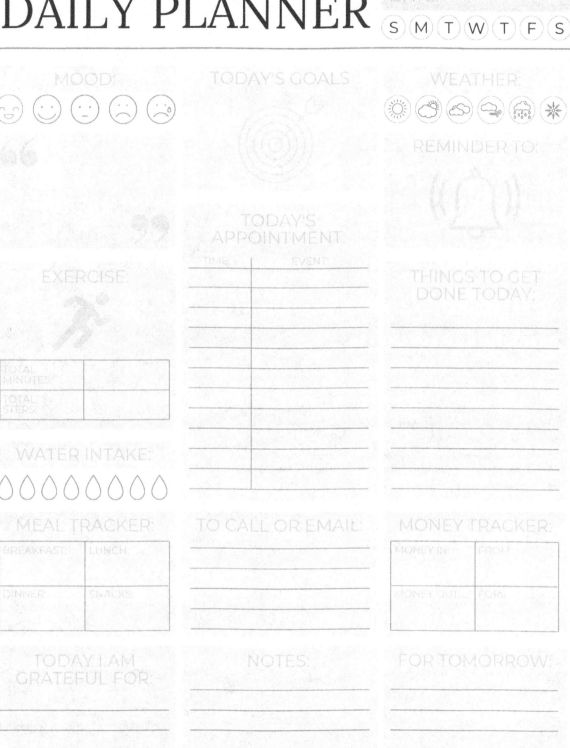

MOOD:

TODAY'S GOALS

WEATHER:

REMINDER TO:

EXERCISE:

TOTAL MINUTES:	
TOTAL STEPS:	

WATER INTAKE:

TODAY'S APPOINTMENT

TIME	EVENT

THINGS TO GET DONE TODAY:

MEAL TRACKER:

BREAKFAST:	LUNCH:
DINNER:	SNACKS:

TO CALL OR EMAIL:

MONEY TRACKER:

MONEY IN:	FROM:
MONEY OUT:	FOR:

TODAY I AM GRATEFUL FOR:

NOTES:

FOR TOMORROW:

I CAN AFFIRMATIONS

HERE ARE 15 "I CAN" AFFIRMATIONS TO HELP YOU OVERCOME FEAR, BROKENNESS, AND DOUBT:

OVERCOMING FEAR:

1. I CAN FACE MY FEARS WITH COURAGE AND CONFIDENCE, KNOWING THAT I AM STRONGER THAN ANY CHALLENGE.
2. I CAN RELEASE THE GRIP OF FEAR ON MY LIFE AND EMBRACE NEW OPPORTUNITIES WITH AN OPEN HEART.
3. I CAN TRANSFORM FEAR INTO FUEL FOR GROWTH AND USE IT AS A STEPPING STONE TO SUCCESS.
4. I CAN TRUST IN MY ABILITIES TO HANDLE ANY SITUATION THAT COMES MY WAY WITH GRACE AND RESILIENCE.
5. I CAN CULTIVATE A MINDSET OF FEARLESSNESS, KNOWING THAT I AM SUPPORTED AND PROTECTED BY THE UNIVERSE.

OVERCOMING BROKENNESS:

6. I CAN HEAL AND MEND THE BROKEN PIECES OF MY HEART, CREATING A STRONGER AND MORE RESILIENT VERSION OF MYSELF.
7. I CAN EMBRACE MY PAST WOUNDS AS VALUABLE LESSONS AND USE THEM TO BUILD A BRIGHTER FUTURE.
8. I CAN FIND STRENGTH IN MY VULNERABILITY, KNOWING THAT IT IS A SIGN OF COURAGE AND AUTHENTICITY.
9. I CAN RELEASE THE PAIN OF BROKENNESS AND EMBRACE THE BEAUTY OF MY IMPERFECTIONS.
10. I CAN REBUILD MY LIFE WITH LOVE AND COMPASSION, KNOWING THAT I AM DESERVING OF HAPPINESS AND WHOLENESS.

OVERCOMING DOUBT:

11. I CAN SILENCE THE VOICE OF DOUBT WITHIN ME AND REPLACE IT WITH UNWAVERING SELF-BELIEF.
12. I CAN TRUST IN MY INTUITION AND MAKE DECISIONS CONFIDENTLY, KNOWING THAT I AM GUIDED BY INNER WISDOM.
13. I CAN LET GO OF SELF-DOUBT AND STEP INTO MY POWER WITH CERTAINTY AND CONVICTION.
14. I CAN CELEBRATE MY ACCOMPLISHMENTS AND RECOGNIZE THE VALUE I BRING TO THE WORLD.
15. I CAN EMBRACE THE JOURNEY OF GROWTH AND TRANSFORMATION, KNOWING THAT DOUBT HAS NO PLACE IN MY PATH.

REPEAT THESE AFFIRMATIONS DAILY, AND LET THEM STRENGTHEN YOUR RESOLVE. TRUST IN YOUR ABILITY TO CREATE POSITIVE CHANGE IN YOUR LIFE AND REMEMBER THAT YOU ARE CAPABLE OF ACHIEVING ANYTHING YOU SET YOUR MIND TO. **AND SO IT IS!**

I can let go of all negativity!

369 – AND SO IT IS ...

Date:

Morning Manifestation:

1
2
3

Visualize it for a minimum of 17 Seconds ideally 34 Seconds.
How does it feel knowing it is yours already?

Afternoon Manifestation:

1
2
3
4
5
6

Visualize it for 51 Seconds, maintaining focus.
How does it feel knowing it is yours already?

Night Manifestation:

1
2
3
4
5
6
7
8
9

Visualize it for 68 Seconds uninterrupted.
How does it feel knowing it is yours already?

Today's Limitless Possibility:

DAILY PLANNER

S M T W T F S

MOOD:

TODAY'S GOALS

WEATHER:

REMINDER TO:

EXERCISE

TOTAL MINUTES	
TOTAL STEPS	

TODAY'S APPOINTMENT

TIME:	EVENT

THINGS TO GET DONE TODAY:

WATER INTAKE:

MEAL TRACKER:

BREAKFAST:	LUNCH:
DINNER:	SNACKS:

TO CALL OR EMAIL:

MONEY TRACKER:

MONEY IN:	FROM:
MONEY OUT:	FOR:

TODAY I AM GRATEFUL FOR:

NOTES:

FOR TOMORROW:

I WILL AFFIRMATIONS

HERE ARE TEN "I WILL" AFFIRMATIONS THAT AFFIRM GRATITUDE, OPENING UP, AND ALLOWING PROSPERITY, HAPPINESS, LOVE, HOPE, AND ABUNDANCE INTO YOUR LIFE:

1. I WILL CULTIVATE A DAILY PRACTICE OF GRATITUDE, APPRECIATING THE BLESSINGS AND ABUNDANCE ALREADY PRESENT IN MY LIFE.

2. I WILL OPEN MY HEART AND MIND TO NEW EXPERIENCES, WELCOMING POSITIVE CHANGE WITH ENTHUSIASM AND CURIOSITY.

3. I WILL ALLOW PROSPERITY TO FLOW INTO MY LIFE EFFORTLESSLY, KNOWING THAT I AM DESERVING OF FINANCIAL ABUNDANCE AND SUCCESS.

4. I WILL CHOOSE HAPPINESS IN EVERY SITUATION, FOCUSING ON THE POSITIVES AND LETTING GO OF NEGATIVITY.

5. I WILL OPEN MYSELF TO GIVING AND RECEIVING LOVE UNCONDITIONALLY, NURTURING MEANINGFUL CONNECTIONS WITH OTHERS.

6. I WILL HAVE HOPE FOR THE FUTURE, KNOWING THAT THE UNIVERSE HAS BEAUTIFUL PLANS IN STORE FOR ME.

7. I WILL EMBRACE OPPORTUNITIES THAT ALIGN WITH MY DESIRES AND VALUES, ALLOWING ABUNDANCE TO MANIFEST IN ALL AREAS OF MY LIFE.

8. I WILL PRACTICE SELF-LOVE AND CARE, KNOWING THAT I AM A MAGNET FOR POSITIVE ENERGY AND WELL-BEING.

9. I WILL REMAIN OPEN TO RECEIVING ABUNDANCE FROM UNEXPECTED SOURCES, TRUSTING THAT THE UNIVERSE ALWAYS PROVIDES.

10. I WILL CREATE A LIFE FILLED WITH JOY, LOVE, AND ABUNDANCE, AND I WILL INSPIRE OTHERS TO DO THE SAME THROUGH MY POSITIVE ENERGY.

REPEAT THESE AFFIRMATIONS REGULARLY AND VISUALIZE THEM AS YOUR REALITY AND YOU WILL ALIGN YOUR MINDSET AND ENERGY WITH THE FREQUENCIES OF GRATITUDE, PROSPERITY, HAPPINESS, LOVE, HOPE, AND ABUNDANCE. AS YOU DO SO, YOU'LL NATURALLY ATTRACT MORE OF THESE POSITIVE EXPERIENCES INTO YOUR LIFE, CREATING A FULFILLING AND JOYOUS JOURNEY. TRUST IN YOUR ABILITY TO CO-CREATE YOUR REALITY, AND REMEMBER THAT YOU HOLD THE POWER TO MANIFEST A LIFE FILLED WITH ALL THAT YOU DESIRE. **AND SO IT IS!**

I can let go of all negativity!

369 – AND SO IT IS ...

Date: _____

Morning Manifestation:

1 _____
2 _____
3 _____

☐ *Visualize it for a minimum of 17 Seconds ideally 34 Seconds.*
How does it feel knowing it is yours already?

Afternoon Manifestation:

1 _____
2 _____
3 _____
4 _____
5 _____
6 _____

☐ *Visualize it for 51 Seconds, maintaining focus.*
How does it feel knowing it is yours already?

Night Manifestation:

1 _____
2 _____
3 _____
4 _____
5 _____
6 _____
7 _____
8 _____
9 _____

☐ *Visualize it for 68 Seconds uninterrupted.*
How does it feel knowing it is yours already?

Today's Limitless Possibility:

DAILY PLANNER

MOOD:

TODAY'S GOALS

WEATHER:

REMINDER TO:

EXERCISE:

TOTAL MINUTES	
TOTAL STEPS	

TODAY'S APPOINTMENT:

TIME	EVENT

THINGS TO GET DONE TODAY:

WATER INTAKE:

MEAL TRACKER:

BREAKFAST	LUNCH
DINNER	SNACKS

TO CALL OR EMAIL:

MONEY TRACKER:

MONEY IN	FROM
MONEY OUT	FOR

TODAY I AM GRATEFUL FOR:

NOTES:

FOR TOMORROW:

TODAY I CHOOSE AFFIRMATIONS

THE POWER OF CHOICE

OUR LIVES ARE LARGELY DEFINED BY THE CHOICES WE MAKE, EACH ONE SHAPING OUR JOURNEY AND ITS OUTCOME. IN A WORLD FULL OF CONSTANT DISTRACTIONS AND EXTERNAL INFLUENCES, IT'S ESSENTIAL TO REMEMBER THE AUTONOMY WE HAVE OVER OUR THOUGHTS, ACTIONS, AND FEELINGS. THE FOLLOWING AFFIRMATIONS REMIND US OF THE POWER WE POSSESS TO MOLD OUR DESTINY:

1. TODAY, I CHOOSE TO EMBRACE THOUGHTS THAT ENHANCE MY LIFE'S QUALITY.
2. TODAY, I CHOOSE TO TAKE ACTIONS THAT UPLIFT AND ENRICH MY LIFE.
3. TODAY, I CHOOSE TO USE WORDS THAT INSPIRE POSITIVITY AND GROWTH IN MY LIFE.
4. TODAY, I CHOOSE TO FOSTER THOUGHTS THAT CONTRIBUTE TO A BETTER WORLD.
5. TODAY, I CHOOSE TO ENGAGE IN ACTIONS THAT CREATE A POSITIVE IMPACT ON THE WORLD.
6. TODAY, I CHOOSE TO SPEAK WORDS THAT PROMOTE HARMONY AND PROGRESS IN THE WORLD.
7. TODAY, I CHOOSE TO SURROUND MYSELF WITH PEOPLE WHO ADD VALUE AND POSITIVITY TO MY LIFE.
8. TODAY, I CHOOSE TO FOLLOW A SPIRITUAL PATH THAT RESONATES DEEPLY WITH MY SOUL.
9. TODAY, I CHOOSE TO EMBRACE A POLITICAL IDEOLOGY THAT WORKS TOWARD A BETTER WORLD.
10. TODAY, I CHOOSE TO LOVE OVER FEAR IN ALL MY INTERACTIONS AND EXPERIENCES.
11. TODAY, I CHOOSE TO HOLD ONTO HOPE AND NEVER GIVE IN TO DESPAIR OR GIVING UP.
12. TODAY, I CHOOSE TO BELIEVE IN ABUNDANCE AND ABUNDANCE-MINDED THINKING.
13. TODAY, I CHOOSE TO PURSUE GROWTH AND CONTINUOUS IMPROVEMENT OVER STAGNATION.
14. TODAY, I CHOOSE TO TAKE DECISIVE ACTION AND AVOID PROCRASTINATION.
15. TODAY, I CHOOSE TO CHERISH AND PROTECT MY FREEDOM, STANDING AGAINST TYRANNY.
16. TODAY, I CHOOSE TO CHASE AFTER MY DREAMS, DISMISSING DOUBTS THAT HOLD ME BACK.
17. TODAY, I CHOOSE TO FORM MY OWN OPINIONS, EMBRACING INDEPENDENT THINKING.
18. TODAY, I CHOOSE TO PICK MY BATTLES WISELY, INVESTING ENERGY IN WORTHY CAUSES.
19. TODAY, I CHOOSE TO FOCUS ON THE GOOD IN HUMANITY AND ITS POTENTIAL FOR GREATNESS.

Today I choose Happiness!

369 – AND SO IT IS ...

Date:

Morning Manifestation:

1
2
3

☐ Visualize it for a minimum of 17 Seconds ideally 34 Seconds.
How does it feel knowing it is yours already?

Afternoon Manifestation:

1
2
3
4
5
6

☐ Visualize it for 51 Seconds, maintaining focus.
How does it feel knowing it is yours already?

Night Manifestation:

1
2
3
4
5
6
7
8
9

☐ Visualize it for 68 Seconds uninterrupted.
How does it feel knowing it is yours already?

Today's Limitless Possibility:

DAILY PLANNER

DATE:

S M T W T F S

MOOD:

TODAY'S GOALS

WEATHER:

REMINDER TO:

EXERCISE:

TOTAL MINUTES:	
TOTAL STEPS:	

TODAY'S APPOINTMENT:

TIME:	EVENT:

THINGS TO GET DONE TODAY:

WATER INTAKE:

MEAL TRACKER:

BREAKFAST:	LUNCH:
DINNER:	SNACKS:

TO CALL OR EMAIL:

MONEY TRACKER:

MONEY IN:	FROM:
MONEY OUT:	FOR:

TODAY I AM GRATEFUL FOR:

NOTES:

FOR TOMORROW:

I DESERVE AFFIRMATIONS

HERE ARE TEN "I DESERVE" AFFIRMATIONS TO ATTRACT LOVE, HAPPINESS, AND ALL THE GOOD LIFE HAS TO OFFER, ALONG WITH HOPE, PROSPERITY, AND ABUNDANCE:

1. I DESERVE TO BE DEEPLY LOVED AND CHERISHED FOR WHO I AM, ATTRACTING A FULFILLING AND LOVING RELATIONSHIP INTO MY LIFE.

2. I DESERVE TO EXPERIENCE TRUE HAPPINESS AND JOY IN EVERY ASPECT OF MY LIFE, EMBRACING POSITIVITY AND GRATITUDE EACH DAY.

3. I DESERVE ALL THE GOOD THAT LIFE HAS TO OFFER, AND I WELCOME ABUNDANT BLESSINGS INTO MY LIFE WITH OPEN ARMS.

4. I DESERVE TO HAVE HOPE AND OPTIMISM FOR THE FUTURE, KNOWING THAT THE BEST IS YET TO COME.

5. I DESERVE TO EXPERIENCE PROSPERITY AND FINANCIAL ABUNDANCE, ATTRACTING WEALTH FROM VARIOUS SOURCES EFFORTLESSLY.

6. I DESERVE TO BE SURROUNDED BY ABUNDANCE IN ALL FORMS, FROM LOVE AND FRIENDSHIPS TO OPPORTUNITIES AND SUCCESS.

7. I DESERVE TO EXPERIENCE A LIFE FILLED WITH ABUNDANCE, WHERE MY DREAMS AND ASPIRATIONS BECOME MY REALITY.

8. I DESERVE TO LIVE A LIFE OF FULFILLMENT AND PURPOSE, MAKING A POSITIVE IMPACT ON THE WORLD AND THOSE AROUND ME.

9. I DESERVE TO ATTRACT AND MANIFEST ALL THE GOOD THAT I DESIRE, TRUSTING THAT THE UNIVERSE CONSPIRES IN MY FAVOR.

10. I DESERVE TO BE HAPPY, LOVED, AND ABUNDANT, AND I AM WORTHY OF ALL THE BLESSINGS LIFE HAS IN STORE FOR ME.

REPEAT THESE AFFIRMATIONS REGULARLY AND BELIEVE IN YOUR WORTHINESS TO RECEIVE ALL THE GOODNESS THAT LIFE HAS TO OFFER. AS YOU AFFIRM YOUR DESERVINGNESS, YOU WILL NATURALLY ALIGN YOURSELF WITH THE POSITIVE ENERGIES OF LOVE, HAPPINESS, HOPE, PROSPERITY, AND ABUNDANCE. EMBRACE THE BELIEF THAT YOU DESERVE A LIFE FILLED WITH JOY AND FULFILLMENT, AND THE UNIVERSE WILL RESPOND IN KIND, BRINGING YOU EXPERIENCES AND OPPORTUNITIES THAT MATCH YOUR HIGHEST DESIRES. AND SO IT IS!

I deserve the best that life has to offer!

369 – AND SO IT IS ...

Date: _____

Morning Manifestation:

1 _____
2 _____
3 _____

☐ *Visualize it for a minimum of 17 Seconds ideally 34 Seconds.*
How does it feel knowing it is yours already?

Afternoon Manifestation:

1 _____
2 _____
3 _____
4 _____
5 _____
6 _____

☐ *Visualize it for 51 Seconds, maintaining focus.*
How does it feel knowing it is yours already?

Night Manifestation:

1 _____
2 _____
3 _____
4 _____
5 _____
6 _____
7 _____
8 _____
9 _____

☐ *Visualize it for 68 Seconds uninterrupted.*
How does it feel knowing it is yours already?

Today's Limitless Possibility:

_____
_____

DAILY PLANNER

    S M T W T F S

MOOD:

TODAY'S GOALS

WEATHER:

REMINDER TO:

EXERCISE:

TOTAL MINUTES:	
TOTAL STEPS:	

TODAY'S APPOINTMENT:

TIME:	EVENT:

THINGS TO GET DONE TODAY:

WATER INTAKE:

MEAL TRACKER:

BREAKFAST:	LUNCH:
DINNER:	SNACKS:

TO CALL OR EMAIL:

MONEY TRACKER:

MONEY IN:	FROM:
MONEY OUT:	FOR:

TODAY I AM GRATEFUL FOR:

NOTES:

FOR TOMORROW:

I EMBRACE AFFIRMATIONS

HERE ARE TEN "I EMBRACE" AFFIRMATIONS THAT AFFIRM CHANGE AND NEW OPPORTUNITIES, NEW RELATIONSHIPS, AND GRATITUDE:

1. I EMBRACE CHANGE WITH AN OPEN HEART AND A POSITIVE MINDSET, KNOWING THAT IT BRINGS GROWTH AND TRANSFORMATION INTO MY LIFE.

2. I EMBRACE NEW OPPORTUNITIES FEARLESSLY, SEIZING THEM AS STEPPING STONES TO SUCCESS AND FULFILLMENT.

3. I EMBRACE THE BEAUTY OF NEW RELATIONSHIPS, ATTRACTING LOVING AND SUPPORTIVE CONNECTIONS INTO MY LIFE.

4. I EMBRACE THE UNKNOWN WITH EXCITEMENT, TRUSTING THAT EVERY EXPERIENCE HOLDS VALUABLE LESSONS AND GROWTH.

5. I EMBRACE GRATITUDE AS A POWERFUL FORCE IN MY LIFE, ACKNOWLEDGING THE ABUNDANCE THAT SURROUNDS ME.

6. I EMBRACE EACH DAY WITH OPTIMISM, FINDING JOY IN THE SIMPLEST OF MOMENTS AND EXPERIENCES.

7. I EMBRACE THE PRESENT MOMENT FULLY, RECOGNIZING IT AS A GIFT THAT ALLOWS ME TO CREATE A BETTER FUTURE.

8. I EMBRACE MY UNIQUE QUALITIES AND TALENTS, KNOWING THAT THEY CONTRIBUTE TO THE TAPESTRY OF MY LIFE'S PURPOSE.

9. I EMBRACE CHALLENGES AS OPPORTUNITIES FOR LEARNING AND EXPANSION, KNOWING THAT I AM CAPABLE OF OVERCOMING THEM.

10. I EMBRACE SELF-LOVE AND SELF-ACCEPTANCE, NURTURING A DEEP SENSE OF APPRECIATION FOR WHO I AM AND WHO I AM BECOMING.

REPEAT THESE AFFIRMATIONS REGULARLY TO ALIGN YOURSELF WITH THE ENERGY OF EMBRACING CHANGE, NEW OPPORTUNITIES, RELATIONSHIPS, AND GRATITUDE. EMBRACING THESE POSITIVE BELIEFS WILL HELP YOU WELCOME POSITIVE SHIFTS INTO YOUR LIFE AND OPEN YOUR HEART TO THE ABUNDANCE THAT SURROUNDS YOU. AS YOU CULTIVATE A MINDSET OF EMBRACING CHANGE AND GRATITUDE, YOU'LL FIND YOURSELF ATTRACTING MORE OF WHAT YOU DESIRE AND CREATING A LIFE FILLED WITH JOY AND FULFILLMENT.

I embrace all that I am.

369 – AND SO IT IS ...

Date:

Morning Manifestation:

1
2
3

☐ Visualize it for a minimum of 17 Seconds ideally 34 Seconds.
How does it feel knowing it is yours already?

Afternoon Manifestation:

1
2
3
4
5
6

☐ Visualize it for 51 Seconds, maintaining focus.
How does it feel knowing it is yours already?

Night Manifestation:

1
2
3
4
5
6
7
8
9

☐ Visualize it for 68 Seconds uninterrupted.
How does it feel knowing it is yours already?

Today's Limitless Possibility:

DAILY PLANNER

S M T W T F S

MOOD:

TODAY'S GOALS

WEATHER:

REMINDER TO:

TODAY'S APPOINTMENT:

TIME	EVENT:

EXERCISE:

TOTAL MINUTES:	
TOTAL STEPS:	

THINGS TO GET DONE TODAY:

WATER INTAKE:

MEAL TRACKER:

BREAKFAST:	LUNCH:
DINNER:	SNACKS:

TO CALL OR EMAIL:

MONEY TRACKER:

MONEY IN:	FROM:
MONEY OUT:	FOR:

TODAY I AM GRATEFUL FOR:

NOTES:

FOR TOMORROW:

How I chose Happiness Today

_____

_____

_____

_____

_____

_____

_____

_____

_____

_____

_____

_____

_____

_____

_____

_____

_____

A Daily Reminder

As you go through your day, remember that every moment offers an opportunity to choose the path that leads towards fulfillment, growth, and happiness. By consciously recognizing these choices and taking control, you can mold your reality into one that you truly desire. Each day is a new canvas, and your choices are the brush strokes that define its beauty. Choose wisely.

I RELEASE AFFIRMATIONS

HERE ARE TEN "I RELEASE" AFFIRMATIONS TO HELP YOU RELEASE JUDGMENT, HOPELESSNESS, FEAR, GRUDGES, AND SELF-DOUBT:

1. I RELEASE ALL JUDGMENTS OF MYSELF AND OTHERS, EMBRACING ACCEPTANCE AND UNDERSTANDING.

2. I RELEASE FEELINGS OF HOPELESSNESS, AND I CHOOSE TO BELIEVE IN THE INFINITE POSSIBILITIES THAT LIFE HOLDS.

3. I RELEASE ALL FEAR THAT HOLDS ME BACK FROM PURSUING MY DREAMS AND LIVING LIFE TO THE FULLEST.

4. I RELEASE ANY GRUDGES AND RESENTMENTS, REPLACING THEM WITH FORGIVENESS AND COMPASSION.

5. I RELEASE SELF-DOUBT, AND I EMBRACE THE CONFIDENCE AND BELIEF IN MY ABILITIES.

6. I RELEASE THE NEED TO CONTROL EVERYTHING AND SURRENDER TO THE NATURAL FLOW OF LIFE.

7. I RELEASE NEGATIVE THOUGHT PATTERNS, REPLACING THEM WITH POSITIVE AND EMPOWERING BELIEFS.

8. I RELEASE ANY LIMITATIONS I HAVE PLACED ON MYSELF, KNOWING THAT I AM CAPABLE OF ACHIEVING GREATNESS.

9. I RELEASE THE PAST AND EMBRACE THE PRESENT MOMENT, KNOWING THAT IT IS THE ONLY MOMENT I HAVE CONTROL OVER.

10. I RELEASE THE NEED FOR EXTERNAL VALIDATION, FINDING WORTH AND VALIDATION WITHIN MYSELF.

REPEAT THESE AFFIRMATIONS REGULARLY TO LET GO OF NEGATIVE EMOTIONS AND BELIEFS THAT NO LONGER SERVE YOU. AS YOU RELEASE JUDGMENT, HOPELESSNESS, FEAR, GRUDGES, AND SELF-DOUBT, YOU'LL MAKE ROOM FOR POSITIVITY, GROWTH, AND SELF-EMPOWERMENT. EMBRACE THE JOURNEY OF RELEASING AND FREEING YOURSELF FROM THESE LIMITATIONS, ALLOWING YOURSELF TO STEP INTO A MORE ABUNDANT AND FULFILLING LIFE. TRUST IN YOUR ABILITY TO LET GO AND CREATE A BRIGHTER FUTURE FILLED WITH LOVE, JOY, AND CONFIDENCE.

I embrace all that I am.

Release List

I release ...

AFFIRM THIS:

I am grateful for the lessons life has taught me, I learn from mistakes and I let go of the past where there are no more lessons learned.

369 – AND SO IT IS ...

Date: _____

Morning Manifestation:

1 _____
2 _____
3 _____

☐ *Visualize it for a minimum of 17 Seconds ideally 34 Seconds.*
How does it feel knowing it is yours already?

Afternoon Manifestation:

1 _____
2 _____
3 _____
4 _____
5 _____
6 _____

☐ *Visualize it for 51 Seconds, maintaining focus.*
How does it feel knowing it is yours already?

Night Manifestation:

1 _____
2 _____
3 _____
4 _____
5 _____
6 _____
7 _____
8 _____
9 _____

☐ *Visualize it for 68 Seconds uninterrupted.*
How does it feel knowing it is yours already?

Today's Limitless Possibility:

_____

DAILY PLANNER

DATE:

S M T W T F S

MOOD:

TODAY'S GOALS

WEATHER:

REMINDER TO:

TODAY'S APPOINTMENT:

TIME	EVENT

EXERCISE:

TOTAL MINUTES:	
TOTAL STEPS:	

THINGS TO GET DONE TODAY.

WATER INTAKE:

MEAL TRACKER:

BREAKFAST:	LUNCH:
DINNER:	SNACKS:

TO CALL OR EMAIL:

MONEY TRACKER

MONEY IN:	FROM:
MONEY OUT:	FOR:

TODAY I AM GRATEFUL FOR:

NOTES:

FOR TOMORROW:

369 – AND SO IT IS ...

Date: _____

Morning Manifestation:

1 _____

2 _____

3 _____

☐ *Visualize it for a minimum of 17 Seconds ideally 34 Seconds.*
How does it feel knowing it is yours already?

Afternoon Manifestation:

1 _____

2 _____

3 _____

4 _____

5 _____

6 _____

☐ *Visualize it for 51 Seconds, maintaining focus.*
How does it feel knowing it is yours already?

Night Manifestation:

1 _____

2 _____

3 _____

4 _____

5 _____

6 _____

7 _____

8 _____

9 _____

☐ *Visualize it for 68 Seconds uninterrupted.*
How does it feel knowing it is yours already?

Today's Limitless Possibility:

_____

_____

DAILY PLANNER

DATE:

S M T W T F S

MOOD:

TODAY'S GOALS

WEATHER:

REMINDER TO:

TODAY'S APPOINTMENT:

TIME	EVENT

EXERCISE:

THINGS TO GET DONE TODAY:

TOTAL MINUTES	
TOTAL STEPS	

WATER INTAKE:

MEAL TRACKER:

TO CALL OR EMAIL:

MONEY TRACKER:

BREAKFAST	LUNCH
DINNER	SNACKS

MONEY IN	FROM
MONEY OUT	FOR

TODAY I AM GRATEFUL FOR:

NOTES:

FOR TOMORROW:

369 – AND SO IT IS ...

Date: _____

Morning Manifestation:

1 _____
2 _____
3 _____

☐ Visualize it for a minimum of 17 Seconds ideally 34 Seconds.
How does it feel knowing it is yours already?

Afternoon Manifestation:

1 _____
2 _____
3 _____
4 _____
5 _____
6 _____

☐ Visualize it for 51 Seconds, maintaining focus.
How does it feel knowing it is yours already?

Night Manifestation:

1 _____
2 _____
3 _____
4 _____
5 _____
6 _____
7 _____
8 _____
9 _____

☐ Visualize it for 68 Seconds uninterrupted.
How does it feel knowing it is yours already?

Today's Limitless Possibility:

_____

_____

DAILY PLANNER

DATE:

S M T W T F S

MOOD:

TODAY'S GOALS

WEATHER:

REMINDER TO:

TODAY'S APPOINTMENT:

EXERCISE:

TIME	EVENT

THINGS TO GET DONE TODAY:

TOTAL MINUTES:	
TOTAL STEPS:	

WATER INTAKE:

MEAL TRACKER:

TO CALL OR EMAIL:

MONEY TRACKER:

BREAKFAST:	LUNCH:
DINNER:	SNACKS:

MONEY IN:	FROM:
MONEY OUT:	FOR:

TODAY I AM GRATEFUL FOR:

NOTES:

FOR TOMORROW:

369 – AND SO IT IS ...

Date: _____

Morning Manifestation:

1 _____

2 _____

3 _____

☐ *Visualize it for a minimum of 17 Seconds ideally 34 Seconds.*
How does it feel knowing it is yours already?

Afternoon Manifestation:

1 _____

2 _____

3 _____

4 _____

5 _____

6 _____

☐ *Visualize it for 51 Seconds, maintaining focus.*
How does it feel knowing it is yours already?

Night Manifestation:

1 _____

2 _____

3 _____

4 _____

5 _____

6 _____

7 _____

8 _____

9 _____

☐ *Visualize it for 68 Seconds uninterrupted.*
How does it feel knowing it is yours already?

Today's Limitless Possibility:

_____

_____

DAILY PLANNER

S M T W T F S

MOOD:

TODAY'S GOALS

WEATHER

REMINDER TO:

EXERCISE:

TODAY'S APPOINTMENT

TIME	EVENT

THINGS TO GET DONE TODAY:

TOTAL MINUTES	
TOTAL STEPS	

WATER INTAKE:

MEAL TRACKER:

BREAKFAST	LUNCH
DINNER	SNACKS

TO CALL OR EMAIL:

MONEY TRACKER:

MONEY IN	FROM

TODAY I AM GRATEFUL FOR:

NOTES:

FOR TOMORROW:

369 – AND SO IT IS ...

Date:

Morning Manifestation:

1
2
3

☐ *Visualize it for a minimum of 17 Seconds ideally 34 Seconds.*
How does it feel knowing it is yours already?

Afternoon Manifestation:

1
2
3
4
5
6

☐ *Visualize it for 51 Seconds, maintaining focus.*
How does it feel knowing it is yours already?

Night Manifestation:

1
2
3
4
5
6
7
8
9

☐ *Visualize it for 68 Seconds uninterrupted.*
How does it feel knowing it is yours already?

Today's Limitless Possibility:

DAILY PLANNER

S M T W T F S

MOOD:

TODAY'S GOALS

WEATHER:

REMINDER TO

TODAY'S
APPOINTMENT:

EXERCISE:

TIME	EVENT

THINGS TO GET
DONE TODAY:

TOTAL MINUTES	
TOTAL STEPS	

WATER INTAKE:

MEAL TRACKER:

BREAKFAST	LUNCH
DINNER	SNACKS

TO CALL OR EMAIL

MONEY TRACKER:

MONEY IN	FROM
MONEY OUT	FOR

TODAY I AM
GRATEFUL FOR:

NOTES:

FOR TOMORROW:

369 – AND SO IT IS ...

Date: _____

Morning Manifestation:

1 _____
2 _____
3 _____

☐ *Visualize it for a minimum of 17 Seconds ideally 34 Seconds. How does it feel knowing it is yours already?*

Afternoon Manifestation:

1 _____
2 _____
3 _____
4 _____
5 _____
6 _____

☐ *Visualize it for 51 Seconds, maintaining focus. How does it feel knowing it is yours already?*

Night Manifestation:

1 _____
2 _____
3 _____
4 _____
5 _____
6 _____
7 _____
8 _____
9 _____

☐ *Visualize it for 68 Seconds uninterrupted. How does it feel knowing it is yours already?*

Today's Limitless Possibility:

_____

DAILY PLANNER

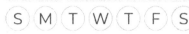

DATE:

S M T W T F S

MOOD:

TODAY'S GOALS

WEATHER:

REMINDER TO:

EXERCISE:

TODAY'S APPOINTMENT:

TIME	EVENT

THINGS TO GET DONE TODAY:

TOTAL MINUTES:	
TOTAL STEPS:	

WATER INTAKE:

MEAL TRACKER:

BREAKFAST:	LUNCH:
DINNER:	SNACKS:

TO CALL OR EMAIL:

MONEY TRACKER:

MONEY IN:	FROM
MONEY OUT:	FOR:

TODAY I AM GRATEFUL FOR:

NOTES:

FOR TOMORROW:

I TRUST IN GOD AFFIRMATIONS

HERE ARE TEN "I TRUST" AFFIRMATIONS TO STRENGTHEN YOUR FAITH IN GOD, ALLOWING HIM TO SUPPLY YOUR NEEDS AND USHER IN A NEW HAPPY LIFE FULL OF LOVE, HOPE, FULFILLMENT, HAPPINESS, AND ABUNDANCE:

1. I TRUST IN GOD'S DIVINE PLAN FOR MY LIFE, KNOWING THAT HE WILL SUPPLY ALL MY NEEDS ACCORDING TO HIS ABUNDANT GRACE.

2. I TRUST IN THE POWER OF FAITH AND BELIEF, ALLOWING GOD TO MANIFEST MIRACLES AND BLESSINGS IN MY LIFE.

3. I TRUST THAT GOD'S LOVE SURROUNDS ME, FILLING MY HEART WITH JOY AND CONTENTMENT.

4. I TRUST IN GOD'S GUIDANCE, KNOWING THAT HE LEADS ME TO A LIFE OF PURPOSE AND FULFILLMENT.

5. I TRUST THAT GOD'S HOPE AND GRACE SUSTAIN ME THROUGH ANY CHALLENGES I MAY FACE.

6. I TRUST IN GOD'S DIVINE TIMING, BELIEVING THAT EVERYTHING UNFOLDS PERFECTLY ACCORDING TO HIS PLAN.

7. I TRUST IN THE ABUNDANCE OF GOD'S BLESSINGS, KNOWING THAT I AM WORTHY OF HIS GOODNESS.

8. I TRUST IN GOD'S UNWAVERING SUPPORT AND LOVE, ALLOWING HIM TO BRING POSITIVE CHANGE INTO MY LIFE.

9. I TRUST IN GOD'S PROMISES, BELIEVING THAT A NEW HAPPY LIFE FULL OF LOVE, HOPE, AND ABUNDANCE AWAITS ME.

10. I TRUST IN GOD'S INFINITE WISDOM, SURRENDERING MY WORRIES AND FEARS, KNOWING THAT HE IS IN CONTROL.

REPEAT THESE AFFIRMATIONS WITH A HEART FULL OF FAITH AND TRUST. AS YOU DEEPEN YOUR CONNECTION WITH GOD AND TRUST IN HIS DIVINE PLAN, YOU'LL FIND PEACE AND REASSURANCE, AND YOUR LIFE WILL BE FILLED WITH LOVE, HOPE, FULFILLMENT, HAPPINESS, AND ABUNDANCE. ALLOW HIS BLESSINGS TO FLOW INTO YOUR LIFE, AND OPEN YOURSELF TO THE NEW AND BEAUTIFUL EXPERIENCES THAT AWAIT YOU ON THIS JOURNEY OF FAITH AND TRUST.

Trust in God's guidance.

369 – AND SO IT IS ...

Date:

Morning Manifestation:

1

2

3

☐ *Visualize it for a minimum of 17 Seconds ideally 34 Seconds.*
How does it feel knowing it is yours already?

Afternoon Manifestation:

1

2

3

4

5

6

☐ *Visualize it for 51 Seconds, maintaining focus.*
How does it feel knowing it is yours already?

Night Manifestation:

1

2

3

4

5

6

7

8

9

☐ *Visualize it for 68 Seconds uninterrupted.*
How does it feel knowing it is yours already?

Today's Limitless Possibility:

DAILY PLANNER

DATE:

S M T W T F S

MOOD:

TODAY'S GOALS

WEATHER:

REMINDER TO:

EXERCISE:

TOTAL MINUTES:	
TOTAL STEPS:	

TODAY'S APPOINTMENT:

TIME:	EVENT:

THINGS TO GET DONE TODAY:

WATER INTAKE:

MEAL TRACKER:

BREAKFAST:	LUNCH:
DINNER:	SNACKS:

TO CALL OR EMAIL:

MONEY TRACKER:

MONEY IN:	FROM:
MONEY OUT:	FOR:

TODAY I AM GRATEFUL FOR:

NOTES:

FOR TOMORROW:

I TRUST AFFIRMATIONS

HERE ARE TEN "I TRUST" AFFIRMATIONS TO STRENGTHEN YOUR FAITH AND CULTIVATE A SENSE OF TRUST IN YOURSELF AND THE UNIVERSE:

1. I TRUST IN THE DIVINE WISDOM THAT GUIDES ME TOWARD MY HIGHEST GOOD.

2. I TRUST THAT EVERYTHING HAPPENS FOR A REASON AND SERVES MY GROWTH AND EVOLUTION.

3. I TRUST IN MY INTUITION, KNOWING THAT IT LEADS ME TO MAKE THE RIGHT DECISIONS.

4. I TRUST IN MY ABILITIES AND KNOW THAT I AM CAPABLE OF OVERCOMING ANY CHALLENGE.

5. I TRUST IN THE POWER OF RESILIENCE, AND I BOUNCE BACK STRONGER FROM LIFE'S SETBACKS.

6. I TRUST IN THE ABUNDANCE OF THE UNIVERSE AND WELCOME PROSPERITY INTO MY LIFE.

7. I TRUST IN THE FLOW OF LIFE, ALLOWING IT TO CARRY ME TOWARD MY DREAMS AND DESIRES.

8. I TRUST IN THE PROCESS OF LIFE, AND I EMBRACE EACH EXPERIENCE WITH AN OPEN HEART.

9. I TRUST IN THE POWER OF LOVE TO HEAL AND TRANSFORM ANY SITUATION.

10. I TRUST THAT THE UNIVERSE SUPPORTS ME, AND I AM ALWAYS GUIDED TOWARD MY HIGHEST GOOD.

REPEAT THESE AFFIRMATIONS REGULARLY WITH CONVICTION AND BELIEF. TRUST IS A POWERFUL FORCE THAT OPENS DOORS TO ENDLESS POSSIBILITIES AND CREATES A DEEP SENSE OF PEACE WITHIN. AS YOU AFFIRM YOUR TRUST IN YOURSELF AND THE UNIVERSE, YOU'LL FIND THAT LIFE ALIGNS WITH YOUR POSITIVE EXPECTATIONS, AND YOU'LL BE BETTER EQUIPPED TO NAVIGATE CHALLENGES WITH GRACE AND CONFIDENCE. TRUST IN THE PROCESS, TRUST IN YOURSELF, AND TRUST IN THE INFINITE POTENTIAL THAT LIFE OFFERS.

I trust in the process of life.

369 – AND SO IT IS ...

Date: _____

Morning Manifestation:

1 _____
2 _____
3 _____

☐ *Visualize it for a minimum of 17 Seconds ideally 34 Seconds.*
How does it feel knowing it is yours already?

Afternoon Manifestation:

1 _____
2 _____
3 _____
4 _____
5 _____
6 _____

☐ *Visualize it for 51 Seconds, maintaining focus.*
How does it feel knowing it is yours already?

Night Manifestation:

1 _____
2 _____
3 _____
4 _____
5 _____
6 _____
7 _____
8 _____
9 _____

☐ *Visualize it for 68 Seconds uninterrupted.*
How does it feel knowing it is yours already?

Today's Limitless Possibility:

_____
_____

DAILY PLANNER

S M T W T F S

MOOD:

TODAY'S GOALS

WEATHER:

REMINDER TO:

EXERCISE:

TODAY'S APPOINTMENT:

TIME:	EVENT

THINGS TO GET DONE TODAY:

TOTAL MINUTES	
TOTAL STEPS	

WATER INTAKE:

MEAL TRACKER:

BREAKFAST	LUNCH
DINNER	SNACK

TO CALL OR EMAIL:

MONEY TRACKER:

MONEY IN	FROM
MONEY OUT	FOR

TODAY I AM GRATEFUL FOR:

NOTES:

FOR TOMORROW:

369 - AND SO IT IS ...

Date: _____

Morning Manifestation:

1 _____
2 _____
3 _____

☐ *Visualize it for a minimum of 17 Seconds ideally 34 Seconds.*
How does it feel knowing it is yours already?

Afternoon Manifestation:

1 _____
2 _____
3 _____
4 _____
5 _____
6 _____

☐ *Visualize it for 51 Seconds, maintaining focus.*
How does it feel knowing it is yours already?

Night Manifestation:

1 _____
2 _____
3 _____
4 _____
5 _____
6 _____
7 _____
8 _____
9 _____

☐ *Visualize it for 68 Seconds uninterrupted.*
How does it feel knowing it is yours already?

Today's Limitless Possibility:

_____
_____

YOUR BLANK CANVAS

Draw your dream life... what does it look like? Visualize it and map it out. Remember, you are a limitless being, and it is already yours!

And so it is!

I AM BECOMING AFFIRMATIONS

BECOMING WHAT YOU SEEK IS ESSENTIAL, HERE ARE SOME I AM BECOMING AFFIRMATIONS SO YOU MAY TRULY BECOME THE NEW VERSION OF YOU!

1. I AM BECOMING A MAGNET FOR LOVE, ATTRACTING MEANINGFUL AND LOVING RELATIONSHIPS INTO MY LIFE EFFORTLESSLY.
2. I AM BECOMING HAPPIER EACH DAY, FINDING JOY IN THE PRESENT MOMENT AND APPRECIATING LIFE'S BLESSINGS.
3. I AM BECOMING A BEACON OF HOPE, INSPIRING OTHERS TO EMBRACE OPTIMISM AND BELIEVE IN BRIGHTER DAYS.
4. I AM BECOMING FREE FROM JUDGMENT AND EMBRACING ACCEPTANCE AND UNDERSTANDING FOR MYSELF AND OTHERS.
5. I AM BECOMING CONFIDENT IN MY ABILITY TO OVERCOME CHALLENGES AND GROW FROM LIFE'S EXPERIENCES.
6. I AM BECOMING A MASTER OF RELEASING NEGATIVE EMOTIONS, FREEING MYSELF FROM FEAR, GRUDGES, AND SELF-DOUBT.
7. I AM BECOMING OPEN TO CHANGE, WELCOMING NEW OPPORTUNITIES AND EXPERIENCES WITH EXCITEMENT.
8. I AM BECOMING GRATEFUL FOR ALL THAT I HAVE, RECOGNIZING THE ABUNDANCE THAT SURROUNDS ME.
9. I AM BECOMING MORE LOVING, SHOWING COMPASSION AND KINDNESS TO MYSELF AND OTHERS.
10. I AM BECOMING MORE RESILIENT, BOUNCING BACK STRONGER FROM ANY SETBACKS THAT COME MY WAY.
11. I AM BECOMING A SOURCE OF HOPE AND INSPIRATION, SHARING OPTIMISM WITH THOSE AROUND ME.
12. I AM BECOMING A CONSCIOUS CREATOR OF MY REALITY, MANIFESTING MY DREAMS AND DESIRES WITH INTENTION.
13. I AM BECOMING MORE ALIGNED WITH MY PURPOSE, LIVING A LIFE OF FULFILLMENT AND MEANING.
14. I AM BECOMING A MASTER OF TRUST, SURRENDERING TO THE FLOW OF LIFE AND BELIEVING IN DIVINE TIMING.
15. I AM BECOMING MORE SKILLED IN THE ART OF RELEASING NEGATIVITY, EMBRACING FORGIVENESS, AND LETTING GO.
16. I AM BECOMING A MAGNET FOR POSITIVE ENERGY, ATTRACTING BLESSINGS AND OPPORTUNITIES WITH MY MINDSET.
17. I AM BECOMING AN EMBODIMENT OF LOVE, SPREADING LOVE AND KINDNESS WHEREVER I GO.

REPEAT THESE AFFIRMATIONS REGULARLY WITH CONVICTION AND BELIEF. AS YOU EMBRACE THE ESSENCE OF THESE "I AM BECOMING" AFFIRMATIONS, YOU'LL EXPERIENCE PROFOUND SHIFTS IN YOUR MINDSET AND ENERGY, LEADING YOU TOWARD A LIFE FILLED WITH LOVE, HAPPINESS, ABUNDANCE, HOPE, TRUST, AND POSITIVE TRANSFORMATION. EMBRACE YOUR JOURNEY OF BECOMING, TRUST IN THE LIMITLESS POTENTIAL WITHIN YOU, AND SO IT IS.

I am becoming a magnet for love.

Crafting Your Personal Power Affirmations

Embarking on a journey of self-discovery often begins with a single word, a phrase, or an idea that deeply resonates within. In this section, you are invited to tap into your inner wisdom, to craft affirmations that are unique to your life, dreams, and aspirations. Every individual's journey is unique, and so should be the words that empower and guide them. So, with an open heart and a clear mind, dive deep, and let's uncover the powerful affirmations that reside within you. Remember, these are your words, your truths. So, make them count.

Write Your Own Personal Power Affirmations

1. I Have ...
2. I Attract ...
3. I Am Becoming ...
4. I Will ...
5. I Choose ...
6. I Am ...
7. I Choose ...
8. I Deserve ...
9. I Trust ...
10. I Release ...

369 – AND SO IT IS ...

Date: _____

Morning Manifestation:

1 _____
2 _____
3 _____

☐ *Visualize it for a minimum of 17 Seconds ideally 34 Seconds.*
How does it feel knowing it is yours already?

Afternoon Manifestation:

1 _____
2 _____
3 _____
4 _____
5 _____
6 _____

☐ *Visualize it for 51 Seconds, maintaining focus.*
How does it feel knowing it is yours already?

Night Manifestation:

1 _____
2 _____
3 _____
4 _____
5 _____
6 _____
7 _____
8 _____
9 _____

☐ *Visualize it for 68 Seconds uninterrupted.*
How does it feel knowing it is yours already?

Today's Limitless Possibility:

DAILY PLANNER

S M T W T F S

MOOD:

TODAY'S GOALS

WEATHER:

REMINDER TO:

EXERCISE:

TODAY'S APPOINTMENT:

TIME	EVENT

THINGS TO GET DONE TODAY:

TOTAL MINUTES	
TOTAL STEPS	

WATER INTAKE:

MEAL TRACKER:

BREAKFAST	LUNCH
DINNER	SNACKS

TO CALL OR EMAIL:

MONEY TRACKER:

MONEY IN	FROM
MONEY OUT	FOR

TODAY I AM GRATEFUL FOR:

NOTES:

FOR TOMORROW:

IT IS ALREADY YOURS

"Whatever we plant in our subconscious mind and nourish with repetition and emotion will one day become a reality."

EARL NIGHTENGALE

CHAPTER 5: IT'S ALREADY YOURS - UNLEASHING THE POWER OF IMAGINATION AFFIRMATIONS FOR ABUNDANCE, HEALTH, WEALTH, HAPPINESS AND FULFILLMENT

In this chapter, we invite you to embark on a journey of self-discovery and empowerment, tapping into the boundless power of your imagination. Within you lies the key to unlocking your ideal life, a life filled with everything your heart desires. The universe has already heard your wishes, and the seeds of your dreams are sown within your very being.

Find a quiet place where you can sit comfortably, free from distractions. Close your eyes, taking a deep breath to center yourself. With each breath, allow the worries of the outside world to dissipate, leaving behind only a sense of peace and tranquility.

Now, in the canvas of your mind, paint a vivid picture of your ideal life. Imagine yourself living that life to the fullest, experiencing every moment with all your senses engaged. Feel the joy, love, and fulfillment coursing through your veins as your dreams come to life.

In this moment of pure imagination, you hold the power to create your future. Everything you could ever want is already within you, waiting to be manifested in your reality. Embrace the feelings of abundance, happiness, and love, knowing that they are your birthright.

As you continue to delve deeper into your imagination, recognize that focusing on negativity will only draw more negativity into your life. Shift your attention to the positive aspects of your ideal life, leaving no room for doubt or fear. Your thoughts hold immense creative power, shaping the reality you will experience.

THE MAGIC OF IMAGINATION

In this present moment, your imagination becomes a magical tool, capable of weaving the tapestry of your dreams into reality. Trust that the universe conspires to bring your desires to fruition, and have faith in your ability to co-create with the universe.

Embrace this sense of empowerment, knowing that you possess the keys to your destiny. With every thought, every intention, and every visualization, you set the wheels of manifestation into motion.

As you open your eyes, carry the essence of this experience with you throughout your day. Whenever doubt or negativity creeps in, return to this moment of imagination and remind yourself that your dreams are already within your grasp.

Remember, you are the author of your story, and the pen is in your hands. Embrace the power of imagination, for in doing so, you unleash the limitless potential of your being. Your ideal life is not a distant dream; it is a reality waiting to be embraced. And so it is.

"The man who has no imagination has no wings." -

MUHAMMAD ALI

CHAPTER 6: 7 POWERFUL MANTRAS TO SHIFT YOUR LIFE

Day 1: I am aligning my inner and outer worlds. I embrace my desires within, independent of my present external circumstances. Releasing all doubt, fear, and stress, I rely on the evidence of my vivid imagination rather than solely on my physical reality. In my inner realm, I satisfy all my wishes, and with joyful anticipation, I witness my external world aligning with my inner vision. And so it is.

Day 2: I embrace the new me, a rebirth of my true desires. With unwavering faith and trust, I rest, satisfied with my inner world's abundant treasures. Doors of opportunity swing open, revealing unseen possibilities that I envision with clarity. I feel the manifestations unfolding, for everything I desire is already mine within my inner world and coming to fruition in my outer world. And so it is.

Day 3: I release all past limitations and step boldly into my power. Limiting beliefs no longer hold sway over my actions and decisions. I am capable of achieving greatness, and I allow my true potential to shine brightly. Each step I take is infused with confidence, and I embrace the limitless possibilities that lie ahead. And so it is.

Day 4: I am a magnet for positive energy and abundant blessings. As I radiate positivity and gratitude, I attract like-minded souls and opportunities that align with my highest good. I am open to receiving all the abundance that the universe has to offer, and I graciously accept the gifts that flow effortlessly into my life. And so it is.

Day 5: I surrender to the divine flow of life. I trust that everything is unfolding in perfect harmony, even when it may not seem so. I release the need to control and allow life to guide me toward my dreams and aspirations. I find peace in surrendering, knowing that the universe is conspiring in my favor. And so it is.

Day 6: I am a beacon of love and compassion. I extend kindness and understanding to myself and others, knowing that we are all on unique journeys. I forgive freely, letting go of any grievances or resentment that weigh me down. Love is my guiding force, and I spread its light wherever I go. And so it is.

Day 7: I am the creator of my reality. I take responsibility for my thoughts, emotions, and actions, knowing that they shape my experiences. I choose to focus on the positive, and I align my intentions with my heart's true desires. With every thought, I am actively shaping a future filled with joy, abundance, and fulfillment. And so it is.

With these powerful mantras, I embrace the transformation within me, opening myself to a life of unlimited possibilities and positive change. I am the author of my destiny, and I am excited to see the beautiful tapestry that unfolds before me. And so it is.

"And the day came when the risk to remain tight in a bud was more painful than the risk it took to blossom."

ANAIS NIN

369 – AND SO IT IS ...

Date:

Morning Manifestation:

1
2
3

☐ *Visualize it for a minimum of 17 Seconds ideally 34 Seconds.*
How does it feel knowing it is yours already?

Afternoon Manifestation:

1
2
3
4
5
6

☐ *Visualize it for 51 Seconds, maintaining focus.*
How does it feel knowing it is yours already?

Night Manifestation:

1
2
3
4
5
6
7
8
9

☐ *Visualize it for 68 Seconds uninterrupted.*
How does it feel knowing it is yours already?

Today's Limitless Possibility:

DAILY PLANNER

  S M T W T F S

MOOD:

TODAY'S GOALS

WEATHER:

REMINDER TO:

EXERCISE:

TOTAL MINUTES	
TOTAL STEPS:	

TODAY'S APPOINTMENT:

TIME:	EVENT:

THINGS TO GET DONE TODAY:

WATER INTAKE:

MEAL TRACKER:

BREAKFAST:	LUNCH:
DINNER:	SNACKS:

TO CALL OR EMAIL:

MONEY TRACKER:

MONEY IN:	FROM:
MONEY OUT:	FOR:

TODAY I AM GRATEFUL FOR:

NOTES:

FOR TOMORROW:

I FEEL AFFIRMATIONS

EMBRACING HOW YOU FEEL IN EVERY MOMENT IS PIVOTAL. DIVE INTO THESE "I FEEL" AFFIRMATIONS TO CHANNEL POSITIVE ENERGIES AND TUNE INTO THE CURRENT VERSION OF YOURSELF:

1. I FEEL LOVE SURROUNDING ME, FILLING EVERY CELL OF MY BEING.
2. I FEEL JOY BUBBLING UP WITHIN ME, TRANSFORMING EVERY CHALLENGE INTO AN OPPORTUNITY.
3. I FEEL THE HOPE THAT LIGHTS UP THE DARKEST MOMENTS, GUIDING ME FORWARD.
4. I FEEL FREE FROM THE CHAINS OF PAST JUDGMENTS, BATHING IN SELF-ACCEPTANCE AND LOVE.
5. I FEEL THE STRENGTH AND COURAGE RISING IN ME, READY TO FACE EVERY CHALLENGE HEAD-ON.
6. I FEEL THE RELEASE OF OLD PAINS AND RESENTMENTS, MAKING ROOM FOR PEACE AND SERENITY.
7. I FEEL AN OPENNESS TO LIFE'S VIBRANT POSSIBILITIES, EMBRACING CHANGE WITH A HEART FULL OF EXCITEMENT.
8. I FEEL A DEEP SENSE OF GRATITUDE, APPRECIATING THE TAPESTRY OF EXPERIENCES THAT MAKE UP MY LIFE.
9. I FEEL AN OVERWHELMING LOVE FOR MYSELF, TREATING MY BODY, MIND, AND SPIRIT WITH GENTLE KINDNESS.
10. I FEEL THE RESILIENCE IN MY BONES, KNOWING THAT I CAN WEATHER ANY STORM AND COME OUT EVEN STRONGER.

INCORPORATE THESE AFFIRMATIONS INTO YOUR DAILY RITUALS. AS YOU GENUINELY FEEL AND RESONATE WITH THESE POWERFUL STATEMENTS, YOU'LL NOTICE AN UPLIFTING CHANGE IN YOUR EMOTIONS AND PERSPECTIVES. HONOR YOUR FEELINGS, CHERISH YOUR JOURNEY, AND WATCH AS THE UNIVERSE ALIGNS WITH YOUR HEART'S TRUE DESIRES. AND SO IT IS.

I feel aligned with the best version of me!

BE WHAT YOU SEEK

"Everyone thinks of changing the world, but no one thinks of changing himself."

LEO TOLSTOY

CHAPTER 7: BEING WHAT YOU WISH TO ATTRACT - THE LAW OF ATTRACTION IN ACTION

IIn this chapter, we explore the profound principle of the Law of Attraction and how it manifests in your life through the art of being what you wish to attract. This powerful concept teaches us that like attracts like, and the energy we emit into the world influences the experiences and people we draw into our reality.

Imagine yourself as a magnet, constantly emitting a magnetic field that draws in energies that resonate with your own. If you desire love, abundance, positivity, and success, you must embody these qualities yourself. You become a living reflection of the desires you hold in your heart.

To be what you wish to attract, you must start within. Cultivate self-love, self-acceptance, and self-worth. As you learn to love and appreciate yourself, you become a beacon of love, attracting loving and supportive relationships into your life.

Focus on cultivating abundance in all areas of your life. Gratitude is a potent force that attracts more blessings and prosperity. Acknowledge the abundance you already have, and watch as it multiplies before your eyes.

Maintain a positive outlook on life, embracing optimism and hope even in challenging times. The energy you exude becomes a magnet for positivity, drawing positive circumstances and people into your path.

Success is born from a mindset of determination and perseverance. Be resilient in the face of obstacles, and let your actions mirror the success you wish to achieve. As you become a person who is dedicated to personal growth and achievement, success will naturally find its way to you.

Embrace kindness, compassion, and understanding towards others. As you extend these qualities to the world, they return to you multiplied. Choose to see the good in others, and you will attract people who bring out the best in you.

In your interactions with the world, choose love over fear. Let go of judgment and replace it with acceptance and empathy. As you radiate love, you will magnetize love into your life.

Remember, you are not merely wishing for these qualities to enter your life; you are becoming the embodiment of them. Your energy aligns with the energy you wish to attract, and this alignment becomes a magnetic force drawing your desires towards you.

As you move through life being what you wish to attract, you will witness the magic of the Law of Attraction in action. Opportunities will present themselves, synchronicities will occur, and you will attract people and circumstances that match the energy you emit.

Embrace this powerful truth, and let it guide your thoughts, actions, and intentions. You hold the power to shape your reality by being the embodiment of your deepest desires. As you radiate positivity, love, abundance, and success, the universe will mirror your energy, delivering to you the life you truly desire. And so it is.

CHAPTER 8: FROM VICTIM TO VICTOR - AFFIRMING YOUR NEW FUTURE

In this chapter, we embark on a powerful transformational journey, shifting from the mindset of a victim to that of a victor. We will delve into the profound practice of affirmations, empowering you to reclaim your personal power and shape a new future filled with resilience, strength, and triumph.

The victim mindset keeps us trapped in a cycle of powerlessness, blame, and despair. It convinces us that external circumstances control our lives and that we have no agency to create change. But in truth, we hold the power to rewrite our narrative and transcend the limitations of victimhood.

Affirmations serve as a bridge between our conscious and subconscious minds, allowing us to reprogram deep-seated beliefs and thought patterns. By affirming empowering statements, we awaken the victor within us - a warrior of courage, determination, and unwavering faith.

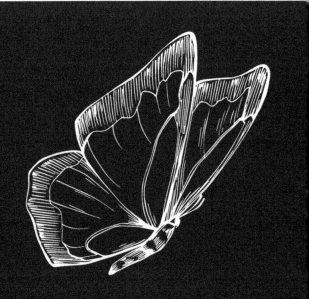

"We are all butterflies. Earth is our chrysalis."

LEEANN TAYLOR

YOU MUST FIRST BELEIVE

"Imagination is the preview of life's coming attractions."

ALBERT EINSTEIN

CHAPTER 9: THE POWER OF 3-6-9 METHOD - HARNESSING THE LAW OF BELIEF FOR MANIFESTATION

In this chapter, we explore the transformative practice of the 3-6-9 method, a powerful technique inspired by Dr. Joseph Murphy's profound quote, "The law of life is the law of belief." This method harnesses the law of belief and aligns our thoughts and intentions with the energy we wish to manifest, amplifying the manifestation process. The 3-6-9 method is a potent technique because it combines the power of repetition with the law of belief to accelerate the manifestation process

The 3-6-9 method is simple yet profound. It involves affirming what you wish to manifest three times a day - in the morning, noon, and night. By repeatedly affirming your desires throughout the day, you reinforce your beliefs and align your energy with the universe's creative forces.

Dr. Joseph Murphy, a renowned author and expert on the power of the subconscious mind, emphasized the significance of belief in shaping our reality. The law of belief states that whatever we deeply believe, consciously or unconsciously, becomes our reality. Our thoughts and beliefs act as powerful magnets, drawing in the experiences and circumstances that resonate with our dominant mindset.

Affirmations are a direct way to program our subconscious mind with positive beliefs and intentions. By repeating affirmations regularly, we rewire our subconscious, replacing limiting beliefs with empowering ones. The 3-6-9 method leverages the frequency of repetition to accelerate this transformation process.

At noon, amidst the hustle and bustle of the day, take a brief break to recenter yourself. Close your eyes, take a few deep breaths, and repeat your affirmations. This practice realigns your focus and reinforces your positive intentions.

In the evening, before you retire to sleep, use the power of your thoughts to plant the seeds of your desires in your subconscious mind. Your subconscious is highly receptive during sleep, making this an opportune time to affirm your intentions. Visualize your desires as already accomplished, and let go of any doubts or worries.

The 3-6-9 method serves two essential purposes. Firstly, it keeps your mind consciously focused on your desires throughout the day. This heightened awareness prevents the mind from wandering into negative thought patterns and reinforces the positive beliefs you wish to cultivate.

Secondly, consistent repetition impresses your affirmations deeply into your subconscious mind. As your subconscious accepts these new beliefs as truth, it starts to shape your reality accordingly. The universe responds to the energy you emit, attracting experiences that align with your dominant thoughts and beliefs.

Remember that patience and consistency are key when using the 3-6-9 method. Trust in the power of your beliefs, and know that the universe is conspiring to bring your desires to fruition. Throughout this book you have learned my types of affirmations, choose the ones that best suit you, or create your own and make your desires specific. Use the following pages in this book to affirm 3 times per day what you desire at a specific time. I recommend using an alarm on your cell phone or aligning it with your schedule so you can remain consistent.

Morning, noon, and night affirm what you wish in writing along with using the affirmations in this book that speak to your spirit and you will see your life begin to shift to the life you desire.

By affirming your desires three times a day, you align your thoughts, beliefs, and intentions with the reality you wish to create. Embrace this practice with faith and conviction, and watch as your dreams begin to manifest before your very eyes. And so it is.

SAMPLE PLAN:

							Jan	Feb	Mar	(Apr)	May	Jun
Su	Mo	(Tu)	We	Th	Fr	Sa	Jul	Aug	Sep	Oct	Nov	Dec

1 2 3 4 5 6 7 9 10 11 12 13 14 15 16 17 (18) 19 20 21 22 23 24 25 26 27 28 29 30 31

08 am	
09 am	*Write my manifestations 3 times*
10 am	
11 am	
12 pm	
1 pm	
2 pm	*Write my manifestations 6 times*
3 pm	
4 pm	
5 pm	
6 pm	*Write my manifestations 9 times*
19 pm	

My Plan:

Su	Mo	Tu	We	Th	Fr	Sa

1 2 3 4 5 6 7 9 10 11 12 13 14 15 16 17 18 19 20 21 22 23 24 25 26 27 28 29 30 31

08 am	
09 am	
10 am	
11 am	
12 pm	
1 pm	
2 pm	
3 pm	
4 pm	
5 pm	
6 pm	
19 pm	

Notes

MANIFEST THE LOVE YOU DESIRE

"Love recognizes no barriers. It jumps hurdles, leaps fences, penetrates walls to arrive at its destination full of hope."

MAYA ANGELOU

CHAPTER 10: MANIFESTING THE LOVE YOU DESIRE - EMBRACE THE POWER OF ATTRACTION

Love is a profound and transformative force that touches every aspect of our lives. In this chapter, we explore the art of manifesting the love you desire, tapping into the powerful energy of attraction to draw in the love that aligns with your heart's truest desires. So it is with love that we embark on this journey of self-discovery and manifestation.

Love begins within, and it is essential to cultivate self-love and a deep sense of worthiness. Affirmations play a pivotal role in this process, as they help you dismantle any barriers that may be hindering the flow of love into your life. Repeat affirmations such as:

1. I am worthy of love and deserve to receive it fully.
2. I am open to giving and receiving love in all its forms.
3. I attract love effortlessly, as I radiate love from within.

As you embrace self-love, the energy you exude will act as a magnet, drawing in the love you desire from others who resonate with your newfound sense of self-worth.

Be clear about the qualities you seek in a partner and the type of relationship you envision. Create affirmations that align with your desires:

4. I attract a partner who cherishes and supports me unconditionally.
5. I am manifesting a relationship filled with trust, communication, and mutual respect.
6. I am magnetizing a love that nourishes my soul and inspires personal growth.

Trust in divine timing and surrender the outcome to the universe. Have faith that the love meant for you will find its way into your life when the time is right. As you repeat affirmations, release any attachment to specific outcomes and allow the universe to work its magic.

Practice gratitude for love in all its forms, whether it's romantic love, love from family and friends, or the love you have for yourself. Gratitude is a powerful energy that amplifies the love in your life and attracts even more love to you.

Visualize yourself in the loving relationship you desire, feeling the emotions, and experiencing the joy of being with your ideal partner. Use affirmations to affirm this reality:

7. I am already in a loving and fulfilling relationship.
8. I see myself sharing beautiful moments of love and connection with my partner.

Trust in the process of manifestation and remain patient. Avoid settling for less than what your heart truly desires, and believe that the universe has a perfect match for you.

As you embody these affirmations and align your energy with the love you desire, the universe conspires to bring you the love that matches your vibrational frequency. Be open to opportunities and encounters that come your way, as they may be stepping stones leading you to the love you seek.

Through the power of affirmations and the law of attraction, you can manifest the love you desire. Embrace the journey with an open heart, and trust that the love you deserve is on its way to you. So it is with love that you welcome the love of your dreams into your life.

Practice writing your own affirmations to attract the love you deserve:

Write Your Own Love Attraction Affirmations

1. I Deserve a Love that is:
2. I Attract a Partner that is ...
3. I Deserve a Relationship that is ...

The relationship wheel ... in the circles of the wheel below, note the qualities of your dream mate:

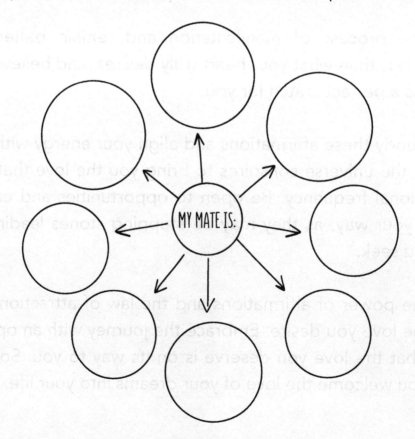

MY MATE IS:

EMBRACE YOUR POWER

"You don't become what you want, you become what you believe."

OPRAH WINFREY

CHAPTER 10: EMBRACING THE POWER WITHIN - A JOURNEY OF TRANSFORMATION THROUGH AFFIRMATIONS

Congratulations on completing this transformative journey through the power of affirmations! As we conclude this chapter, let us reflect on the profound wisdom and insights we have explored thus far.

Throughout this book, we discovered that affirmations are much more than mere words; they are potent tools that have the ability to shape our reality. By aligning our thoughts, beliefs, and intentions with the energy we wish to attract, we become co-creators of our destiny.

In "Sweet Inspirations for the Soul," we explored various types of affirmations that encompassed love, happiness, abundance, hope, trust, release, and embracing change. Each affirmation served as a stepping stone on our journey of self-discovery and empowerment.

We witnessed the power of "I am" affirmations, as they empowered us to embody our desires and embrace the truth of our being. By choosing affirmations that reflected our true desires and focusing on the positive aspects of life, we shifted our mindset toward growth and transformation.

"The most common way people give up their power is by thinking they don't have any." -

ALICE WALKER

We embraced the concept of "I have" affirmations, acknowledging the abundance that already surrounds us and aligning our energy with prosperity and fulfillment.

"I attract" affirmations taught us the art of opening ourselves to joy, love, and abundance by becoming magnetic to the energies we wish to experience.

"I can" affirmations helped us overcome fear, doubt, and brokenness, recognizing our limitless potential to overcome challenges and achieve our goals.

"I will" affirmations empowered us to take charge of our destiny, affirming gratitude, opening up to prosperity, love, hope, and abundance, and taking inspired action towards our dreams.

"I choose" affirmations encouraged us to make conscious decisions that lead us towards personal growth, positivity, love, hope, and a brighter future.

"I deserve" affirmations reminded us that we are deserving of love, happiness, and all the good life has to offer, paving the way for a life of fulfillment and abundance.

"I embrace" affirmations encouraged us to embrace change, new opportunities, relationships, and gratitude, allowing positive shifts to unfold in our lives.

"I release" affirmations empowered us to let go of judgment, hopelessness, fear, grudges, and self-doubt, making room for positivity, growth, and self-empowerment.

"I trust" affirmations deepened our faith in ourselves and the universe, allowing us to surrender to the flow of life and manifest a new happy life full of love, hope, and abundance.

We explored the importance of gratitude, recognizing that gratitude is the key that unlocks a world of positivity, abundance, and joy. By cultivating gratitude, we transform our outlook on life and attract more blessings into our reality.

We delved into the power of self-perception and self-talk, understanding that the only opinion that truly matters about us is our own. By mastering self-perception and shifting our self-talk to become a better version of ourselves, we align with a reality that reflects our true worth and potential.

As you close this chapter, remember that you hold the power to shape your reality. Affirmations are your guiding light, illuminating the path to a life filled with love, happiness, abundance, and fulfillment. Embrace the journey of transformation, and know that the power to create a life beyond your wildest dreams lies within you.

May you carry the essence of these affirmations with you as you navigate life's journey, radiating positivity and embracing the sweet inspirations that await you. Trust in the magic of the universe and your limitless potential to create a life that aligns with your deepest desires. **And so it is.**

"Life's journey is not to arrive at the grave safely in a well-preserved body, but rather to skid in sideways, totally worn out, shouting, 'Wow! What a ride!'" —

GUIDED MEDITATION

(AVAILABLE ON AUDIBLE AND ON THE SWEET INSPIRATIONS YOUTUBE CHANNEL AT WWW.YOUTUBE.COM/SWEETINSPIRATIONS)

WELCOME TO THIS GUIDED MEDITATION, A JOURNEY OF SELF-DISCOVERY AND EMPOWERMENT THROUGH AFFIRMATIONS. FIND A COMFORTABLE POSITION, EITHER SITTING OR LYING DOWN, AND CLOSE YOUR EYES. TAKE A DEEP BREATH IN, AND AS YOU EXHALE, RELEASE ANY TENSION IN YOUR BODY. ALLOW YOURSELF TO BE FULLY PRESENT IN THIS MOMENT.

INHALE DEEPLY ONCE AGAIN, FILLING YOUR LUNGS WITH FRESH ENERGY, AND AS YOU EXHALE, LET GO OF ANY LINGERING THOUGHTS OR DISTRACTIONS. YOU ARE HERE, IN THIS SACRED SPACE, READY TO EMBRACE THE POWER OF AFFIRMATIONS.

AS YOU JOURNEY THROUGH THIS MEDITATION, REMEMBER THAT YOU ARE THE CREATOR OF YOUR REALITY. YOUR THOUGHTS AND BELIEFS SHAPE YOUR EXPERIENCES. LET US BEGIN BY AFFIRMING THE ESSENCE OF THIS TRANSFORMATIVE JOURNEY.

You are the architect of your destiny!

REPEAT AFTER ME:

1. I AM THE ARCHITECT OF MY DESTINY, AND I SHAPE MY REALITY WITH POSITIVE INTENTION.
2. I AM WORTHY OF LOVE, ABUNDANCE, AND FULFILLMENT IN ALL ASPECTS OF MY LIFE.
3. I EMBRACE THE POWER OF GRATITUDE, AND IT AMPLIFIES THE BLESSINGS IN MY LIFE.

AS WE DELVE DEEPER, VISUALIZE YOURSELF IN A STATE OF PURE EMPOWERMENT, EMBRACING THE AFFIRMATIONS THAT RESONATE WITH YOUR SOUL. FEEL THE ENERGY OF THESE AFFIRMATIONS PULSATING THROUGH EVERY CELL OF YOUR BEING, IGNITING A FLAME OF TRANSFORMATION WITHIN YOU.

4. I RELEASE THE OLD AND EMBRACE THE NEW, STEPPING INTO THE BEST VERSION OF MYSELF.
5. I AM THE MASTER OF MY THOUGHTS, AND I CHOOSE TO FOCUS ON POSITIVITY AND GROWTH.
6. I ATTRACT ABUNDANCE EFFORTLESSLY, AS I ALIGN MY ENERGY WITH PROSPERITY.

IMAGINE A BRIGHT LIGHT OF MANIFESTATION GLOWING WITHIN YOU, ILLUMINATING YOUR PATH AND GUIDING YOU TOWARDS YOUR HEART'S DESIRES. WITH EACH AFFIRMATION, THIS LIGHT EXPANDS, ILLUMINATING YOUR ENTIRE BEING WITH BOUNDLESS LOVE AND POSSIBILITIES.

7. I AM COURAGEOUS AND RESILIENT, TURNING OBSTACLES INTO STEPPING STONES.
8. I AM OPEN TO NEW OPPORTUNITIES, AND I WELCOME THE GIFTS OF THE UNIVERSE.
9. I AM A VICTOR, RISING ABOVE ANY CIRCUMSTANCES THAT SEEK TO HOLD ME BACK.

FEEL THE POWER OF YOUR WORDS, AND KNOW THAT THE UNIVERSE HEARS YOUR INTENTIONS. EMBRACE THE TRUTH THAT YOU HAVE THE POWER TO SHAPE YOUR REALITY AND CO-CREATE A LIFE FILLED WITH LOVE, JOY, AND ABUNDANCE.

10. I AM A MAGNET FOR LOVE, AND I ATTRACT LOVING RELATIONSHIPS INTO MY LIFE.
11. I AM IN HARMONY WITH THE FLOW OF LIFE, TRUSTING IN DIVINE TIMING.
12. I AM GRATEFUL FOR ALL THE LOVE AND BLESSINGS IN MY LIFE.

AS YOU BASK IN THIS ENERGY OF ABUNDANCE AND NEW POSSIBILITIES, KNOW THAT YOU HOLD THE KEY TO YOUR DESTINY. YOU ARE A POWERFUL CO-CREATOR WITH THE UNIVERSE, AND THROUGH AFFIRMATIONS, YOU ALIGN YOURSELF WITH THE ABUNDANCE THAT IS YOUR BIRTHRIGHT.

TAKE A MOMENT TO EXPRESS GRATITUDE FOR THIS TRANSFORMATIVE JOURNEY AND THE NEW POSSIBILITIES IT HAS OPENED UP FOR YOU. WHEN YOU ARE READY, GENTLY BRING YOUR AWARENESS BACK TO THE PRESENT MOMENT. WIGGLE YOUR FINGERS AND TOES, AND TAKE ONE FINAL DEEP BREATH.

AS YOU OPEN YOUR EYES, CARRY THE ESSENCE OF THESE AFFIRMATIONS WITH YOU THROUGHOUT YOUR DAY. EMBRACE THE POWER WITHIN, AND WATCH AS YOUR REALITY SHIFTS TO ALIGN WITH THE TRUTHS YOU HAVE AFFIRMED. YOU ARE A BEACON OF LIGHT, YOU ARE JOY, YOU ARE POSSIBILITY PERSONIFIED, YOU ARE A GIFT TO THE WORLD AND YOUR LIFE IS FILLED WITH ABUNDANCE. AND SO IT IS.

"May your compass always guide you towards growth, understanding, and the boundless horizons of transformation. Trust in the journey you're crafting, for every step is a testament to your evolution. You are the captain of the ship, your words affirm it's path. My your journey be a beautiful one my friend. Know that whatever it is you truly desire is already yours!
And so it is."

— AUTHOR, MENTOR AND VISIONARY - JOYCE LICORISH

THANK YOU...

As the final page turns and you reach the end of this journey, I want to pause and send my heartfelt gratitude to you. Thank you for inviting this book into your life, for allowing these words to resonate, and for embracing the transformation within yourself. Your commitment to personal growth and self-discovery is inspiring, and it's been an honor to be a small part of your journey.

While this book concludes, our connection does not have to. I invite you to join our community online, share your stories, and continue this journey with us. Connect with fellow readers and be part of an ongoing conversation about transformation, growth, and the incredible power within each of us. Stay updated with our upcoming projects, events, and resources by visiting our website and subscribing to our newsletter.

From the deepest corners of my heart, thank you. Remember, every ending is but a new beginning. Here's to your journey, your transformation, and to the power of affirmation. I declare that your best days lay ahead of you and not behind you, What God has for you, is still for you! Now is all we have, so remember, day one starts today! And so it is.

This book and many other titles by Joyce Licorish are available in eBook, Paperback, Hardback, on Amazon and Audiobook on Audible.

Connect with Joyce also on YouTube at www.YouTube.com/SweetInspirations

Keep in touch

www.DreamEmpirePublishing.com | www.DreamEmpireFilms.com

Joyce Licorish is available for speaking engagements, appearances and bookings.

🌐 www.JoyceLicorish.com

✉ dreamempirepublishing@gmail.com

🌐 IG: @SweetestMotivation | TikTok @JoyceLicorish

✉ dreamempirepublishing@gmail.com

Made in the USA
Monee, IL
19 September 2023

42932045R00083